Research Reports on College Transitions | No. 4

2012-2013 National Survey of First-Year Seminars:

Exploring High-Impact Practices in the First College Year

Dallin George Young and Jessica M. Hopp

Cite as:

Young, D. G., & Hopp, J. M. (2014). *2012-2013 National Survey of First-Year Seminars: Exploring high-impact practices in the first college year* (Research Reports No. 4). Columbia, SC: University of South Carolina, National Resource Center for The First-Year Experience & Students in Transition.

ISBN 978-1-889271-90-3
Published by
National Resource Center for The First-Year Experience® and Students in Transition
University of South Carolina
1728 College Street, Columbia, SC 29208
www.sc.edu/fye

Production Staff for the National Resource Center
Project Manager: Tracy L. Skipper, Assistant Director of Publications
Design & Production: Allison Minsk, Graphic Artist
External Reviewers: Ryan D. Padgett, University of Northern Kentucky; Barbara F. Tobolowsky, University of Texas at Arlington

---

Library of Congress Cataloging-in-Publication Data

Young, Dallin George.
2012-2013 national survey of first-year seminars : exploring high-impact practices in the first college year / by Dallin George Young and Jessica M. Hopp.
pages cm. -- (Research reports on college transitions ; no. 4)
ISBN 978-1-889271-90-3
1. College student orientation--United States--Evaluation. 2. Educational evaluation. I. Hopp, Jessica M.
LB2343.32.Y67 2014
378.1'98--dc23

2013048690

About the Publisher

The National Resource Center for The First-Year Experience and Students in Transition was born out of the success of University of South Carolina's much-honored University 101 course and a series of annual conferences on the freshman-year experience. The momentum created by the educators attending these early conferences paved the way for the development of the National Resource Center, which was established at the University of South Carolina in 1986. As the National Resource Center broadened its focus to include other significant student transitions in higher education, it underwent several name changes, adopting the National Resource Center for The First-Year Experience and Students in Transition in 1998.

Today, the Center collaborates with its institutional partner, University 101 Programs, in pursuit of its mission to advance and support efforts to improve student learning and transitions into and through higher education. We achieve this mission by providing opportunities for the exchange of practical and scholarly information as well as the discussion of trends and issues in our field through the convening of conferences and other professional development events, such as institutes, workshops, and online learning opportunities; publishing scholarly practice books, research reports, a peer-reviewed journal, electronic newsletters, and guides; generating, supporting, and disseminating research and scholarship; hosting visiting scholars; and maintaining several online channels for resource sharing and communication, including a dynamic website, listservs, and social media outlets.

The National Resource Center serves as the trusted expert, internationally recognized leader, and clearinghouse for scholarship, policy, and best practice for all postsecondary student transitions.

Institutional Home

The National Resource Center is located at the University of South Carolina's (USC) flagship campus in Columbia. Founded in 1801, USC Columbia's mission is twofold: (a) to establish and maintain excellence in its student population, faculty, academic programs, living and learning environment, technological infrastructure, library resources, research and scholarship, public and private support, and endowment; and (b) to enhance the industrial, economic, and cultural potential of the state. The Columbia campus offers 324 degree programs through its 14 degree-granting colleges and schools. Students have been awarded more than $16.7 million for national scholarships and fellowships since 1994. In fiscal year 2013, faculty generated $220 million in funding for research, outreach, and training programs. Carolina is one of only 63 public universities listed by the Carnegie Foundation in the highest tier of research institutions in the United States.

Contents

List of Tables and Figures

Tables

Figures

Introduction

Every three years since 1988, the National Resource Center for The First-Year Experience and Students in Transition has conducted a nationwide survey to collect data on first-year seminars. It has been our intention to understand a complex and diverse collection of curricular initiatives aimed at fostering active participation in learning and student development in the first college year. Through the administrations of the National Survey of First-Year Seminars (NSFYS), we have sought to explore, monitor, and provide information on the overall national landscape of first-year seminar programming. This effort has not been fruitless. Over the past quarter century, the results of the NSFYS have yielded the development of a definition and typology of first-year seminars and information about the prevalence of these courses and their characteristics in higher education institutions across the nation. The survey has led the way for an extensive body of research "establish[ing] the first-year seminar as one of the most important instructional vehicles for achieving the learning and developmental objectives of undergraduate education in the United States" (Padgett & Keup, 2011, p. 3).

What Have We Learned From the NSFYS?

The 2012-2013 NSFYS is the ninth triennial administration of the survey, and represents the 25th anniversary of this data collection effort. So, what have we learned about the seminar over the past 25 years? In addition to defining the first-year seminar, the survey has focused broadly on the following aspects of the course: (a) types of seminars offered, (b) characteristics, (c) students in the seminar, (d) instructors, (e) course content, (f) educationally effective pedagogies, and assessment. What follows is a selection of topical areas providing a glimpse of the trends related to the components and features of first-year seminars at a national level over several administrations of the NSFYS.

Defining the First-Year Seminar

The first administrations of the NSFYS were exploratory. The 1988 NSFYS developed a baseline estimate of the prevalence of the seminar nationwide. Subsequent administrations have suggested a steady increase in the number of institutions offering some form of first-year seminar, from 68% in 1988 to 87% in 2009.

A standard and still widely used definition and typology for first-year seminars came out of the early data collection efforts connected to the NSFYS. Barefoot (1992), after reviewing descriptions for nearly 500 courses, defined the first-year seminar generally as "a course intended to enhance the academic and/or social integration of first-year students" (p. 49). She also identified the following five basic types of seminars:

1. ***Extended orientation seminars***. Oftentimes called freshman orientation, college survival, college transition, or student success course, these courses include an introduction to campuses resources, time management, academic and career planning, learning strategies, and to student development concerns.
2. ***Academic seminars with generally uniform academic content across sections.*** This type may be an interdisciplinary or theme-oriented course and sometimes is part of a general education requirement.

The primary focus is an academic theme or discipline but will often include academic skills components, such as critical thinking and expository writing.

3. ***Academic seminars on various topics.*** This seminar's content is similar to the previously mentioned academic seminar except that specific topics vary from section to section.
4. ***Preprofessional seminars or discipline-linked seminar.*** These seminars are designed to prepare students for the demands of the major or discipline and the profession and are oftentimes taught within specific disciplines, professional schools, or majors.
5. ***Basic study skills seminars.*** Generally offered to academically underprepared students, these seminars focus on basic academic skills, such as grammar, note taking, test-taking strategies, and critical-reading techniques.

This typology has proven to be a valuable classification scheme for first-year seminars and continues to be the one most commonly used today. Some institutions offer hybrid seminars, or combinations of the types described above. To capture the prevalence of these courses, hybrid seminars were introduced as a sixth type in the 2006 administration of the survey.

Types of First-Year Seminars

Extended orientation seminars have been the most frequently reported type of first-year seminar since the typology was introduced in the 1991 administration. In more recent administrations, there have been changes in the prevalence of the types of seminars being offered based on institutional characteristics and needs. For example, in the 2000 NSFYS administration, Hunter and Linder (2005) identified a shift toward traditional academic content in the seminar based on a decrease in the percentage of extended orientation courses and an increase in seminars focused on academic content. Since then, while the overall percentage of institutions reporting extended orientation seminars as one type of seminar available on campus has remained relatively steady, the proportion of institutions offering academically focused first-year seminars has increased.

Seminar Grading and Credit

There has been variation over time in the academic status of the course, specifically in how the seminar has been graded and how academic credit has been applied. Findings from the NSFYS have indicated that the percentage of institutions offering a letter grade for the first-year seminars has gradually gone up from 62% in 1988 to 80% in 2009 (Padgett & Keup, 2011). Similarly, more institutions reported applying credits from the course toward major requirements in 2009 (9.7%) than in 1991 (2.4%), when the question was introduced on the survey (Padgett & Keup, 2011; Tobolowsky & Associates, 2008). The application of seminar credit toward general education requirements has increased slightly (from 48.1% in 1991 to 53.1% in 2009) while credits offered as electives decreased (45.4% in 1991 to 39.8% in 2009).

Students Required to Take the Seminar

There has been a slight increase in the number of institutions requiring the seminar for all first-year students, from 43% in 1988 to 54% in 2009 (Padgett & Keup, 2011). In the 2009 administration, four-year institutions were significantly more likely to report requiring the entire first-year class to participate in a first-year seminar than two-year institutions (Padgett & Keup, 2011). Additionally, there has been some interest in which student groups are required to take a first-year seminar. The flexibility of content in seminars affords institutions the ability to address the specific needs of a wide range of students (Padgett & Keup, 2011). The most frequently identified group of students required to enroll in first-year seminars has been those who are academically underprepared or admitted on a provisional basis (Padgett & Keup, 2011; Tobolowsky, 2005; Tobolowsky & Associates, 2008).

Instruction in the Seminar

Since 1988, the number of institutions involving faculty members in the instruction of first-year seminars has continued to increase (Hunter & Linder, 2005). The 2009 administration asked respondents to further delineate the professional role of faculty instructors of the course (i.e., tenure track, full-time nontenure track, adjunct). Most campus respondents marked multiple categories for this survey item, and the analysis showed that full-time faculty were most likely to have seminar teaching responsibilities (Padgett & Keup, 2011).

Educationally Effective Practices in the Seminar

First-year seminars serve as a curricular anchor for other first-year initiatives, as many seminars today are linked to other educationally effective practices on campus, such as common reading experiences, living-learning communities, and service-learning (Greenfield, Keup, & Gardner, 2013). The 1994 administration of the NSFYS was the first investigation into the linking of first-year seminars to other courses in a learning community (Barefoot & Fidler, 1996; Hunter & Linder, 2005). The proportion of institutions reporting that they offer first-year seminars linked with other courses doubled from 1994 (17.2%) to 2009 (35.7%). Over time, questions about seminars including a service-learning component and incorporating a first-year or summer reading program component were included in the NSFYS.

Since 1986, the National Resource Center for The First-Year Experience and Students in Transition has been providing scholarship, resources, and support to these programs as well as those professionals working to enhance the first-year student experience. It has been the Center's focus to explore the national landscape and examine the changes occurring within it. As social changes occur and new academic trends emerge, the first-year seminar is likely to continue to support students at this critical transition point. During times of financial hardship, budget cuts, and curricular change, it is especially important to prove the worth and value of first-year seminars in higher education. Research and assessment continue to be important for the future of first-year seminars, as these evidence-gathering activities can help set all types of seminars down the right path toward long-term success.

The 2012-2013 NSFYS

This retrospective on the findings of the past 25 years of administering the survey leads to the following question: Why conduct the 2012-2013 NSFYS? The ongoing effort to provide a comprehensive and current national snapshot of the state of this initiative might be, in itself, enough of a rationale to continue administering the survey on a regular cycle. As the NSFYS has been administered since 1988, there is real value in our ability to identify trends related to the seminar. In this administration, as in previous efforts, we were concerned with learning more about the current state of the types of seminars, the instruction, the objectives, and other structural characteristics of the course. Yet, what did we hope to learn that we did not yet know? We changed the way we asked about the use of undergraduate peer leaders to find better information regarding their presence and role in the seminar. We were especially concerned with the connection and inclusion of certain educationally purposeful practices in the first-year seminar, such as service-learning, common reading programs, and learning communities. Much attention and discussion in the higher education community has focused on these and other approaches since the American Association of Colleges and Universities (AAC&U) labeled them high-impact practices (AAC&U, 2007; Kuh, 2008). To that end, we included a specialized module that asked institutions to provide information about these high-impact practices and their roles in the first-year seminar. Finally, we were interested in hearing from institutions that do not currently offer a seminar. We asked respondents representing these campuses to identify why they did not currently offer such a course, whether they had ever offered one, and if they were considering implementing one in the future.

Reporting the Results of the 2012-2013 NSFYS

Unlike the 2009 research report, which provided an overview of the results of the majority of items included in the NSFYS, the 2012-2013 report focuses its presentation on fewer items of interest. The decision to call out and discuss fewer items was influenced by several priorities. First, as we reviewed reports of previous administrations of the NSFYS, certain features of the seminar have changed little. Decisions about which results to explore in greater depth were driven by identifying those aspects of the seminar that seemed to be in flux, allowing us to describe the current state of practice in seminars.

The first-year seminar has served as a curricular anchor for a number of educationally effective practices (Greenfield et al., 2013). This administration was designed to investigate high-impact educational practices, as defined by AAC&U (2007), associated with the first-year seminar. These high-impact practices included service-learning, learning communities, common intellectual experiences, writing-intensive experiences, and undergraduate research, among others. Reducing the emphasis on the analysis in other areas of the survey gave us the opportunity to explore this area in more depth.

The research report on the 2009 administration of the NSFYS (Padgett & Keup, 2011) expanded the section of implications for practice over previous reports. Here, we continued our commitment to expand the discussion of the results to provide more guidance for practice and research. In particular, this report explores the results as they relate to contingent faculty as instructors, the rigor of the first-year seminar, the use of undergraduate peer leaders, and the degree to which high-impact practices are intentionally incorporated into seminars.

To that end, the report is organized around the following sections: (a) an overview of the sample of the respondents to the 2012-2013 NSFYS; (b) a review of the results relating to selected characteristics of the first-year seminar, including the types of first-year seminars being offered, student enrollment in seminars, course structure, content, and instructional practices; (c) a description of high-impact practices incorporated in the course; and (d) a discussion of the results and their implications for practice and for future research.

Understanding that readers will bring their own questions and priorities to this volume, we have included the frequency distributions of responses to all questions on the NSFYS in the tables included in Appendix D. These distributions are disaggregated by institutional characteristics (i.e., type, control, entering first-year class size) and primary seminar type. The frequency tables presented in this report are useful tools. Institutions with established seminars can use them for benchmarking purposes, and campuses considering creating a course will find them helpful in exploring possibilities for structuring the seminar.

Description of the Sample

The 2012-2013 National Survey of First-Year Seminars (NSFYS) was administered from November 2012 through January 2013. A total of 3,753 institutions were invited to participate in the survey. The final number of campuses responding with information about the presence of a first-year seminar was 896, representing an effective response rate of 23.9%. This is in line with expected rates from web-based education surveys, which are around 25% (Gunn, 2002; Wang, Dziuban, & Moskal, 2000), and slightly less than the two previous online administrations of the NSFYS (Padgett & Keup, 2011; Tobolowsky & Associates, 2008). Despite this, the low response rate presents a limitation in this research.

Table 1 shows a comparison of the sample of all responding campuses and those who report offering one or more first-year seminars to a national profile of institutions in the United States. The frequencies reported in this table demonstrate that four-year institutions are overrepresented in the sample of respondents. Similarly, the sample includes a greater proportion of campuses with more than 1,000 first-year students than national percentages. Private, for-profit institutions were vastly underrepresented in the sample of responding institutions.

Table 1
Comparison of Institutional Characteristics for Responding Institutions

Institutional characteristic	National percentages	Percentage of all campuses responding to NSFYS (*N* = 896)	Percentage of NSFYS sample with first-year seminars
Control			
Public	36.8	54.1	54.5
Private, not for profit	37.0	42.9	42.8
Private, for profit	26.2	3.0	2.7
Type			
Two-year	48.6	26.7	25.6
Four-year	51.4	73.3	74.4
Number of first-year students			
Less than 500 students	57.5	29.8	29.5
501-1,000 students	20.6	22.8	22.6
1,001-1,500 students	8.9	11.8	11.9
1,501-2,000 students	4.4	7.6	7.5
2,001-2,500 students	2.6	6.6	6.8
2,501-3,000 students	1.7	2.9	2.9
3,001-3,500 students	1.1	4.1	4.5
3,501-4,000 students	1.0	2.5	2.2
4,001-5,000 students	1.1	3.6	3.7
More than 5,000 students	1.1	8.4	8.3

Note. Figures for the national percentages are from The Carnegie Classification of Institutions of Higher Education by the Carnegie Foundation for the Advancement of Teaching, n.d., and The Integrated Postsecondary Education Data System by the National Center for Education Statistics, 2013.

Because of the small number of private, for-profit responding institutions, the categories representing both types of private institutions (not-for-profit and for-profit) have been combined for the remainder of the report. We acknowledge that there are important distinctions between private institutions that operate for profit and those that do not. However, there were so few responses from private, for-profit institutions that comparisons could not be made with confidence on many of the variables. It is possible that the inclusion of for-profit institutions in the private category may slightly skew the results. Yet with these institutions representing less than 10% of the responses in this group, it is unlikely that they would have a confounding effect on the results.

Number of Students in Entering First-Year Class

As the size of the first-year class size increases, the number of four-year institutions in the sample generally decreases (Figure 1). A similar, though less pronounced, distribution is seen among two-year institutions. With the exception of responding campuses with less than 500 students in the incoming first-year class, the distribution of the sample when disaggregated by institutional type mirrors the overall distribution of respondents.

An examination of the entering first-year class size of the sample broken down by institutional control reveals that the majority of private institutions are small (Figure 2). Approximately 80% of private institutions report incoming first-year class sizes of less than 1,000 students. Public institutions with larger numbers of first-year students responded with greater frequency than their private counterparts.

Even with a sample of 804 institutions, cell size decreases rapidly when responses are divided among 10 categories representing size and then again among available response options. To facilitate analysis and interpretation of responses related to size of the first-year class, the 10 categories representing the number of entering students have been collapsed to five: (a) Less than 500; (b) 501-1,000; (c) 1,001-2,000; (d) 2,001-4,000; and (e) More than 4,000. These collapsed categories will be used for the remainder of the report.

Institutions Offering a First-Year Seminar

Of the 896 institutions that responded, 804 (89.7%) offered at least one first-year seminar. While this figure is consistent with the two previous administrations of this survey (Padgett & Keup, 2010, Tobolowsky & Associates, 2008), it represents the highest proportion of colleges and universities reporting the presence of a first-year seminar on campus on any of the previous administrations of the NSFYS. It is reasonable to expect that more institutions with first-year seminars would respond to this survey, thus creating an inflated approximation of the prevalence of the seminar. However, in a national survey of undergraduate programs, Barefoot, Griffin, and Koch (2012) found a higher incidence, with 96.5% of four-year colleges reporting some type of first-year seminar, compared to 91.0% of four-year institutions in the 2012-2013 administration.

Institutions Not Offering a First-Year Seminar

Approximately 10% of respondents ($n = 92$) indicated that, at the time of the survey, their institution did not offer a first-year seminar or that they did not know whether the institution had such a course. Of these institutions, 37.8% noted their campus had, at some point in the past, offered one or more first-year seminars. Disaggregating this group by institutional type revealed that fewer two-year institutions (25.0%) than four-year institutions (44.8%) reported ever offering a seminar. When broken down by control, more public colleges and universities (42.2%) indicated that a seminar once existed on campus than did private campuses (33.3%).

The two reasons most frequently cited for not currently offering a seminar were lack of funding and lack of staff or faculty buy-in, though the majority of institutions identified some other reason for not offering a seminar (Table 2). These responses included such obstacles as a lack of human and facilities resources, no room in the curriculum for such a course, and the emphasis on other programs to support students in the first year. Approximately one quarter of the responses to other indicated that the institutions are conducting research and assessment in preparation for the development of a first-year seminar on campus.

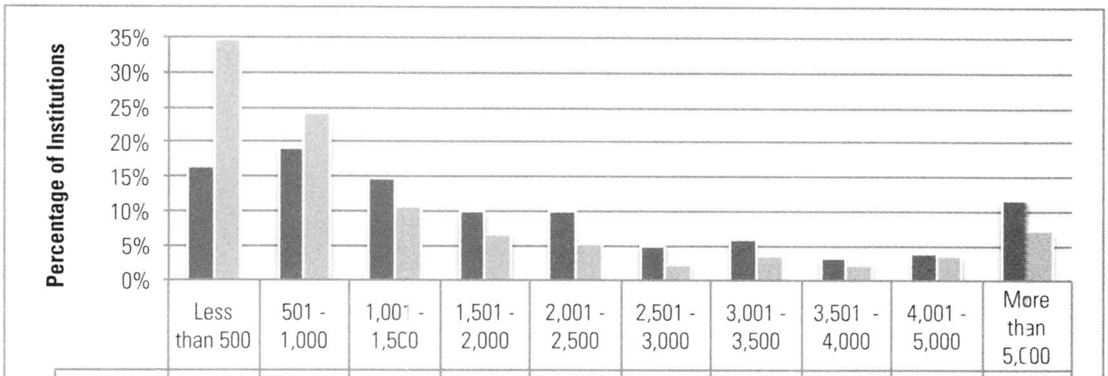

	Less than 500	501 - 1,000	1,001 - 1,500	1,501 - 2,000	2,001 - 2,500	2,501 - 3,000	3,001 - 3,500	3,501 - 4,000	4,001 - 5,000	More than 5,000
Two-year	16.32%	19.25%	14.64%	10.04%	10.04%	5.02%	5.86%	3.35%	3.77%	11.72%
Four-year	34.70%	24.05%	10.81%	6.70%	5.33%	2.13%	3.50%	2.13%	3.50%	7.15%

Figure 1. Number of entering first-year students by institutional type ($N = 896$).

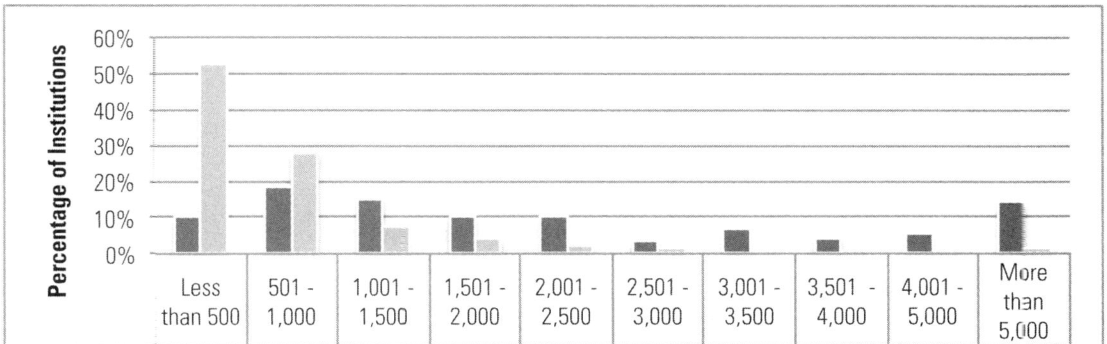

	Less than 500	501 - 1,000	1,001 - 1,500	1,501 - 2,000	2,001 - 2,500	2,501 - 3,000	3,001 - 3,500	3,501 - 4,000	4,001 - 5,000	More than 5,000
Public	10.3%	18.6%	15.3%	10.5%	10.1%	3.9%	7.2%	4.3%	5.8%	14.0%
Private	52.8%	27.7%	7.8%	4.1%	2.4%	1.7%	0.5%	0.2%	1.0%	1.7%

Figure 2. Number of entering first-year students by institutional control ($N = 896$).

Table 2

Reasons First-Year Seminars Are Not Currently Offered

Response	Frequency	Percent
Lack of funding	34	37.8
Lack of staff or faculty buy-in	32	35.6
Limited time	18	20.0
First-year issues are not an institutional priority	10	11.1
Lack of expertise	5	5.6
Other	42	46.7

Conclusion

Small institutions (1,000 or fewer first-year students) and private, for-profit institutions were underrepresented in the 2012-2013 NSFYS sample. In addition, four-year and large institutions were overrepresented. Thus, while the sample is not an exact national representation of U.S. colleges and universities, the distribution of respondents is similar to previous administrations of the survey. Furthermore, the 2012-2013 NSFYS represents the most current and comprehensive national picture of practices related to the first-year seminar. As such, the data and the analyses provide some evidence of the curricular efforts institutions across the United States are making to support students in the first college year.

Characteristics of the First-Year Seminar

Since its inception in 1988, the National Survey of First-Year Seminars (NSFYS) has sought to provide the most up-to-date national and comprehensive examination of first-year seminar features, administration, instruction, and practices. This section provides an overview of selected characteristics of the seminar, focusing on the types of first-year seminars being offered, student enrollment in seminars, course structure, content, and instructional practices.

Seminar Types

Institutions were asked two questions about the type of first-year seminar offered. The first question asked respondents to identify all types of first-year seminars offered (i.e., discrete types of the seminar). As illustrated in Figure 3, the most frequently reported discrete seminar type was extended orientation (60.4%), consistent with previous administrations of the NSFYS. Extended orientation seminars are useful in equipping students with the college success skills that will serve them throughout the remainder of their journey through higher education. In this type of seminar, students learn important lessons in time management, relationship building, the availability of campus resources, and the overall expectations of being a college or university student. The continued prominence of the extended orientation course type reinforces the seminar's role on the majority of campuses as an important tool for supporting incoming students' transition into higher education.

Academic seminars of both types, uniform and variable content, were each offered on approximately 30% of responding campuses (29.4% for academic - uniform content and 28.7% for academic - various topics). This represents an increase of 3.6% in prevalence of academic - uniform content and 5.3% for academic - various topics from the 2009 administration (Padgett & Keup, 2011).

The second question about seminar type asked institutions to indicate which one had the highest student enrollment and was, thus, the primary type of first-year seminar on campus. Figure 4 presents the percentage distribution of primary seminar types. Similar to the distribution of discrete seminar types, extended orientation was the most frequently reported primary seminar type (39.1%). The percentage of institutions identifying extended orientation as the primary seminar has held steady over the two previous administrations of the NSFYS in 2009 (41.1%) and 2006 (40.9).

Academic seminars were reported as the primary seminar on campuses with similar frequencies: 19.2% offered academic - various topics, and 19.0% offered academic - uniform content. When combined, academic seminars were nearly as prevalent as the extended orientation seminar, 38.2% compared to 39.1%. This represents an increase over the two previous administrations, as the combined total percentage in 2009 was 31.5% and 35.3% in 2006.

Some interesting findings emerge when the primary type of first-year seminar is disaggregated by institutional type and control (Figure 5). Two-year colleges offered extended orientation and basic study skills seminars at significantly higher rates than four-year institutions ($p < .001$). In fact, two-year campuses reported the basic study skills seminar as the primary type over eight times more frequently than four-year schools. Conversely, four-year institutions offered academic seminars on various topics eight times more frequently than two-year colleges. Four-year campuses were also nearly twice as likely to report hybrid seminars as the primary type. While four-year institutions were also twice as likely to report preprofessional or discipline-linked seminars as a primary type, the number of two-year campuses reporting this as a primary seminar was small ($n = 4$). Thus, we recommend exercising caution when interpreting this difference.

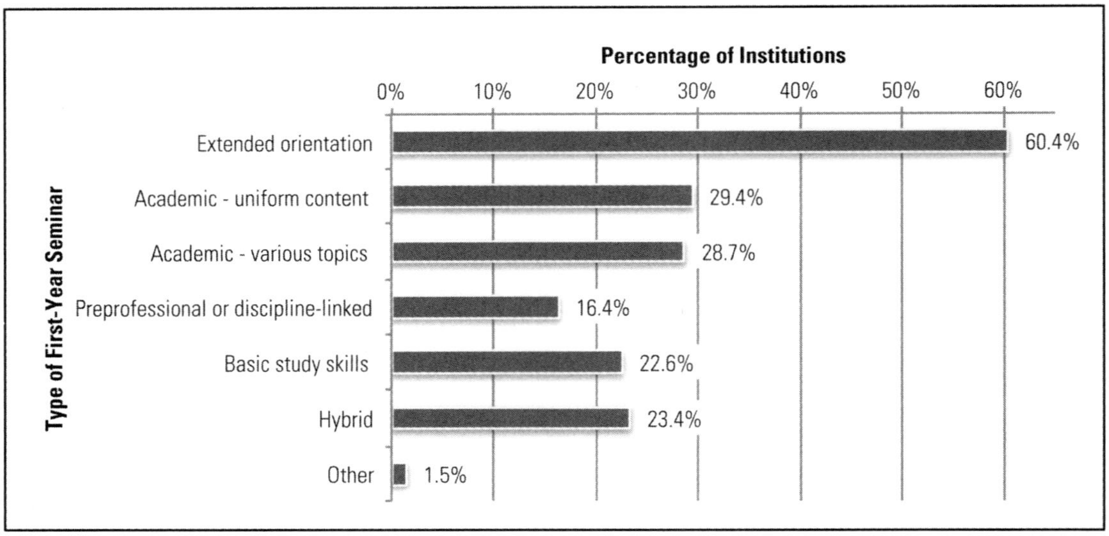

Figure 3. Discrete types of first-year seminars offered ($n = 788$). The sum of the percentages is larger than 100% due to the ability of respondents to select more than one response.

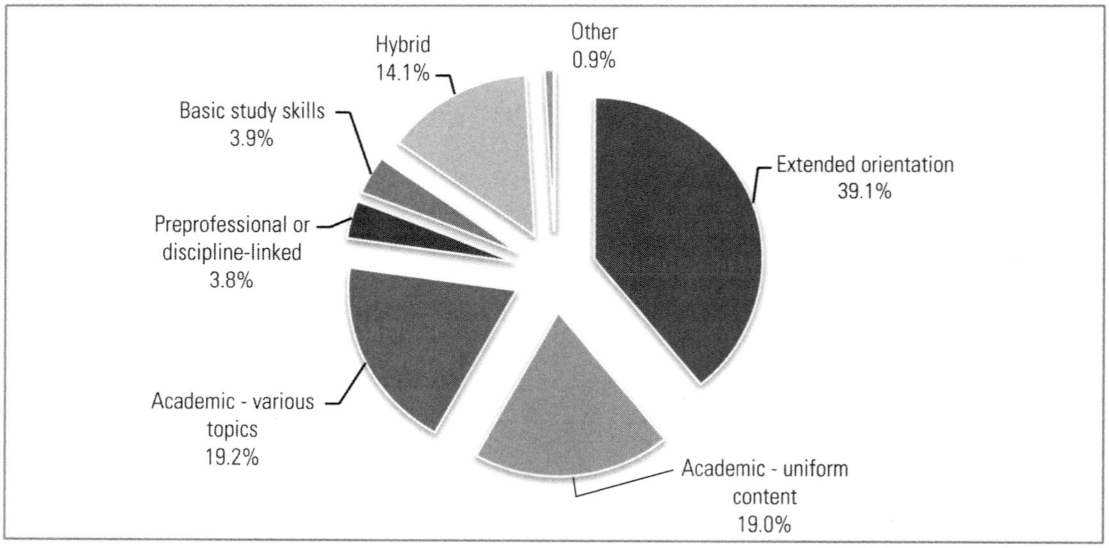

Figure 4. Primary types of first-year seminars offered ($n = 786$).

Disaggregating the primary seminar type by institutional control revealed a similar pattern between public and private institutions, though the differences were not as pronounced as they were with institutional type. Public institutions were significantly more likely to offer extended orientation, preprofessional or discipline-linked, and basic study skills seminars as the primary type ($p < .001$). Public colleges and universities reported offering basic study skills in a proportion nearly three times that of private campuses. The private institutions in the sample were significantly more likely to report that academic seminars on various topics and hybrid seminars were the primary types on their campuses ($p < .001$). Again, similar to institutional type, the proportion of respondents who identified academic seminars with uniform content as the primary type was approximately the same when broken down by institutional control.

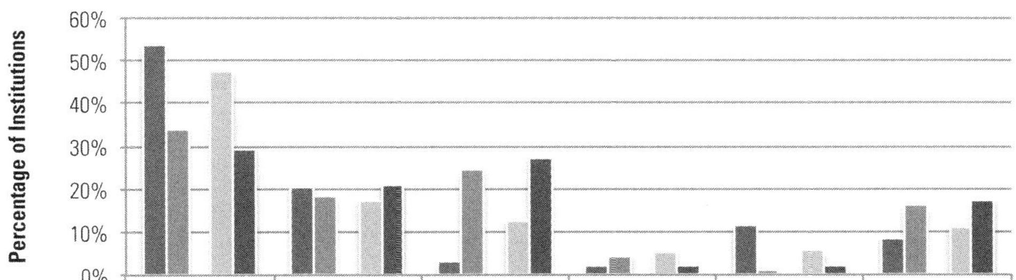

	EO	A-UC	A-VT	PP-D	BSS	HY
Two-year	54.0%	20.5%	3.0%	2.0%	11.5%	8.5%
Four-year	34.0%	18.4%	24.7%	4.4%	1.4%	16.0%
Public	47.4%	17.4%	12.4%	5.4%	5.6%	11.3%
Private	29.2%	20.8%	27.2%	1.9%	1.9%	17.5%

Primary Seminar Type

Figure 5. Primary first-year seminar type by institutional type and control (n = 786). EO = extended orientation, A-UC = academic – uniform content, A-VT = academic – various topics, PP-D = preprofessional or discipline-linked, BSS = basic study skills, HY = hybrid.
$p < .001$.

Student Enrollment Patterns

Respondents were asked three questions about the enrollment of students in first-year seminars on campus: (a) *What is the approximate percentage of first-year students who take a first-year seminar on your campus?* (b) *What is the approximate percentage of first-year students required to take the first-year seminar?* and (c) *Which students, by category, are required to take the first-year seminar?* Responses to these questions for the 2012-2013 administration of the NSFYS yielded somewhat contradictory information. When asked about the requirement to take the first-year seminar (i.e., question b), 333 institutions responded that 100% of students were required to enroll in the seminar. However, when asked which students were required to take the seminar (i.e., question c), 439 institutions responded *all first-year students.* This discrepancy is further compounded when compared to the 270 institutions indicating that 100% of their first-year students are enrolled in a first-year seminar (i.e., question a). The contradictory nature of these responses is even more pronounced because questions (b) and (c) explicitly refer to the primary seminar type while (a) refers to all first-year students on campus. Thus, it would logically follow that the number of responses would be much smaller for (b) and (c); yet, the pattern is the opposite. An investigation of the tables of the 2009 administration of the NSFYS revealed a similar response pattern (Padgett & Keup, 2011). As a result, the findings presented below concerning the enrollment patterns in the first-year seminar should be interpreted with caution.

More than half of all of respondents reported that at least 90% of their students were enrolled in first-year seminars of any type. Figure 6 presents the percentage of students enrolled in the seminar disaggregated by institutional type. More students were enrolled in first-year seminars in four-year institutions than two-year institutions. While approximately 65% of four-year institutions reported that 90% or more of their students are enrolled in a first-year seminar, only 16% of two-year institutions indicated the same. This disparity is potentially due to the fact that four-year institutions are more likely to be residential and to cater to a traditional, full-time first-year student. However, large numbers of students at two-year campuses are enrolling in first-year seminars. More than a half of two-year institutions indicated that at least 50% of their students were enrolled in first-year seminars.

A similar and even more pronounced difference was present when responding institutions were disaggregated by institutional control, as displayed in Figure 7. Nearly 84% of private institutions indicated that 90% or more of their students enroll in a first-year seminar compared to 27% of public institutions. This includes 61% of private institutions that reported 100% of their students enrolled in a first-year seminar.

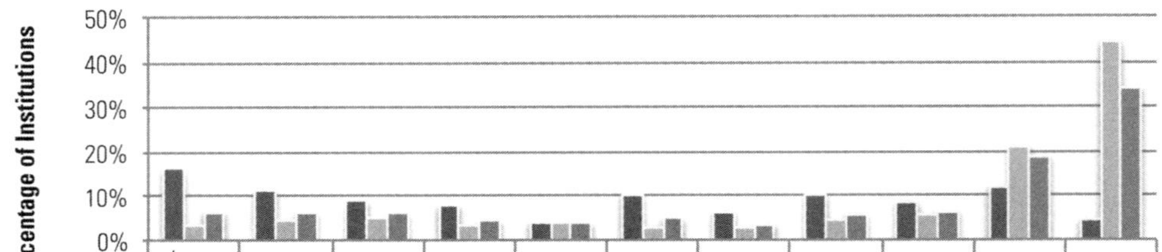

	Less than 10%	10 - 19%	20 - 29%	30 - 39%	40 - 49%	50 - 59%	60 - 69%	70 - 79%	80 - 89%	90- 99%	100%
Two-year	16.3%	11.3%	8.9%	7.9%	3.9%	10.3%	6.4%	10.3%	8.4%	11.8%	4.4%
Four-year	3.1%	4.2%	4.9%	3.2%	3.7%	2.9%	2.5%	4.2%	5.6%	21.2%	44.3%
Total	6.4%	6.1%	5.9%	4.4%	3.8%	4.8%	3.5%	5.8%	6.3%	18.8%	34.1%

Percentage of Students Enrolled in a Seminar

Figure 6. Percentage of students enrolled in a first-year seminar by institutional type (*n* = 792).

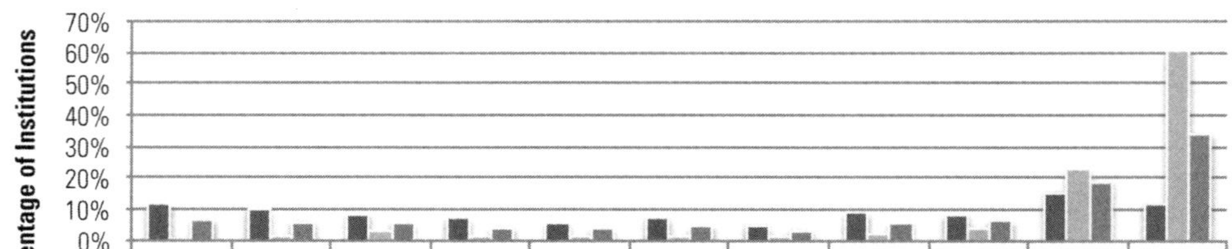

	Less than 10%	10 - 19%	20 - 29%	30 - 39%	40 - 49%	50 - 59%	60 - 69%	70 - 79%	80 - 89%	90- 99%	100%
Public	11.4%	10.0%	8.6%	7.2%	5.8%	7.4%	5.1%	8.8%	8.4%	15.6%	11.6%
Private	0.6%	1.4%	2.8%	1.1%	1.4%	1.7%	1.7%	2.2%	3.9%	22.7%	60.8%
Total	6.4%	6.1%	5.9%	4.4%	3.8%	4.8%	3.5%	5.8%	6.3%	18.8%	34.1%

Percentage of Students Enrolled in a Seminar

Figure 7. Percentage of students enrolled in a first-year seminar by institutional control (*n* = 792).

Students Required to Take Seminar

The NSFYS asked institutions to identify the percentage of students required to take the primary first-year seminar[1] on their campuses. Of the responding institutions, 42.5% reported that all first-year students were required to enroll in the seminar. Further, 55.9% of all institutions required more than 90% of their first-year students to enroll, and 67.2% required more than half to take the seminar.

When disaggregated by institutional type, distinct patterns emerged. The distribution of the percentage of students required to enroll in the seminar at two-year colleges is slightly bimodal with institutions grouped at the two extremes (Figure 8). In other words, 31.1% of two-year campuses required fewer than 10% of their students to take a first-year seminar, and 25.2% required 90% of first-year students to enroll. The distribution of four-year campuses revealed that many more four-year campuses required all first-year students to enroll in the first-year seminar. A majority (51.9%) of four-year institutions required all students to enroll in first-year seminars, while 66.5% required more than 90% of first-year students to enroll in the course. An examination of the distribution of four-year institutions also showed an accumulation at the lower extreme. Of responding four-year campuses, 18.7% required fewer than 10% of students take the first-year seminar.

[1] From this point forward, all questions and responses refer to the primary first-year seminar that was offered on a campus. The online questionnaire was developed to provide a prompt at the top of each screen reminding to respondents to base answers on the seminar type they indicated as having the highest enrollment of students.

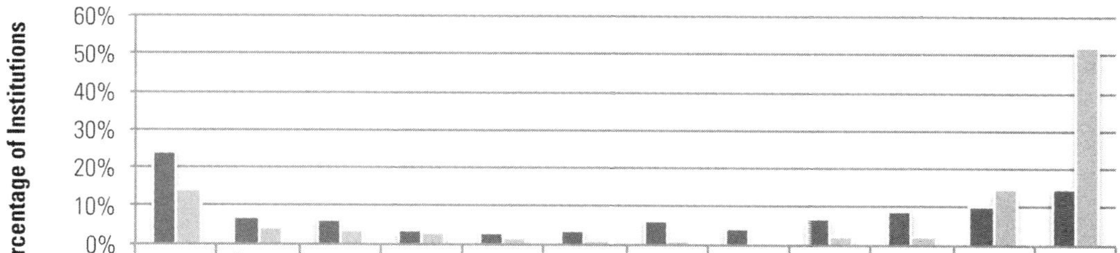

	None	Less than 10%	10 - 19%	20 - 29%	30 - 39%	40 - 49%	50 - 59%	60 - 69%	70 - 79%	80 - 89%	90 - 99%	100%
Two-year	24.1%	7.0%	6.5%	3.5%	3.0%	3.5%	6.5%	4.5%	7.0%	9.0%	10.1%	15.1%
Four-year	14.2%	4.5%	3.8%	2.9%	1.5%	0.9%	0.9%	0.7%	2.1%	2.2%	14.6%	5[illegible].9%

Percentage of Students Required to Take a Seminar

Figure 8. Percentage of students required to take a first-year seminar by institutional type ($n = 783$).
$p < .001$

The distribution of public institutions based on the percentage of first-year students required to enroll in the first-year seminars, as appears in Figure 9, is bimodal with the responses grouped at the two extremes. First-year students at public institutions appeared to be equally likely to be required to take the seminar as not, with nearly a third (33.5%) of respondents requiring fewer than 10% to enroll and the same proportion requiring more than 90% take the course. Private institutions were much more likely to require the seminar, with 65.5% requiring all first-year students to enroll and 80% requiring the course of more than 90% of students.

	None	Less than 10%	10 - 19%	20 - 29%	30 - 39%	40 - 49%	50 - 59%	60 - 69%	70 - 79%	80 - 89%	90 - 99%	100%
Public	25.5%	8.0%	7.3%	4.2%	3.5%	2.6%	3.5%	2.6%	5.0%	4.2%	10.4%	23.1%
Private	6.4%	1.7%	1.1%	1.7%	0.0%	0.3%	0.8%	0.6%	1.4%	3.6%	17.0%	65.5%

Percentage of Students Required to Take a Seminar

Figure 9. Percentage of students required to take a first-year seminar by institutional control ($n = 783$).
$p < .001$

Categories of Students Required to Take Seminar

Respondents were asked to identify specific categories of students who are required to take the first-year seminar. The three most frequently reported categories were (a) academically underprepared students (12.5%), (b) students within specific majors (7.9%), and (c) students enrolled in developmental or remedial courses (7.1%). An additional 10.0% of institutions identified other groups of students required to enroll in the seminar, including students in STEM majors, provisionally admitted students, students from groups historically underrepresented in higher education, and students who received scholarships. Many of the responses described other groups of students who were exempt from the requirement, such as honors students, transfer students, and nontraditional students.

When disaggregated by institutional characteristics, results showed that four-year institutions and private institutions were more likely to require all students to enroll in seminars (Tables 3 and 4). Noteworthy is that private institutions reported requiring all first-year students at a proportion nearly twice that of public institutions, 86.9% compared to 47.0% ($p < .001$). Four-year and private institutions were more likely to have 100% of their first-year class enrolled in the seminar, which may explain why requirements for specific populations were more prevalent at public and two-year institutions.

At public and two-year institutions, which are less likely to require all students to take a first-year seminar, students specifically targeted to enroll in a first-year seminar are predominantly those who might not be considered college-ready (e.g., academically underprepared, enrolled in developmental courses, provisionally admitted). At public institutions in particular, students participating in support programs, such as TRIO and learning communities, are more likely to be required to enroll in a first-year seminar. It is probable that participation in a learning community is also required for students who are enrolled in developmental education courses (see discussion on learning communities in the "High-Impact Practices in the First-Year Seminar" section).

Table 3

Categories of Students Required to Enroll in a First-Year Seminar by Institutional Type ($n = 649$)

	Institutional type					
	Two-year		Four-year			
Catergory of student	Freq.	%	Freq.	%	Difference (%)	p
Percentages larger for two-year institutions						
Academically underprepared students	42	28.0	39	7.8	20.2	***
Students enrolled in developmental or remedial courses	31	20.7	15	3.0	17.7	***
Other	24	16.0	41	8.2	7.8	**
Students within specific majors	20	13.3	31	6.2	7.1	**
Transfer students	4	2.7	2	0.4	2.3	a
First-generation students	6	4.0	10	2.0	2.0	
TRIO participants	7	4.7	16	3.2	1.5	
Students participating in dual-enrollment programs	2	1.3	1	0.2	1.1	a
Student athletes	6	4.0	16	3.2	0.8	
Learning community participants	8	5.3	23	4.6	0.7	
Honors students	3	2.0	10	2.0	0.0	
Percentages larger for four-year institutions						
All first-year students are required to take it	64	42.7	375	75.2	-32.5	***
Provisionally admitted students	3	2.0	29	5.8	-3.8	
Undeclared students	0	0.0	17	3.4	-3.4	a
International students	1	0.7	9	1.8	-1.1	
Preprofessional students	2	1.3	12	2.4	-1.1	
Students residing within a particular residence hall	0	0.0	5	1.0	-1.0	a

Note. If *All first-year students are required to take it* was selected, respondents could not select other responses. Additionally, institutions indicating that no students were required to take a first-year seminar were not able to respond to this question due to the skip logic of the online questionnaire.

[a]Analysis was not conducted due to cell counts less than five.

$^{**}p < .01$. $^{***}p < .001$.

Table 4

Categories of Students Required to Enroll in a First-Year Seminar by Institutional Control (n = 649)

Category of student	Public Freq.	Public %	Private Freq.	Private %	Difference (%)	p
Percentages larger for public institutions						
Academically underprepared students	71	22.7	10	3.0	19.7	***
Students within specific majors	42	13.4	9	2.7	10.7	***
Students enrolled in developmental or remedial courses	39	12.5	7	2.1	10.4	***
Other	46	14.7	19	5.7	9.0	***
Learning community participants	25	8.0	6	1.8	6.2	***
Provisionally admitted students	23	7.3	9	2.7	4.7	**
Student athletes	18	5.8	4	1.2	4.6	a
TRIO participants	18	5.8	5	1.5	4.3	**
Undeclared students	13	4.2	4	1.2	3.0	a
Honors students	9	2.9	4	1.2	1.7	a
First-generation students	10	3.2	6	1.8	1.4	
Preprofessional students	8	2.6	6	1.8	0.8	
Transfer students	4	1.3	2	0.6	0.7	a
Students residing within a particular residence hall	3	1.0	2	0.6	0.4	a
Students participating in dual-enrollment programs	2	0.6	1	0.3	0.3	a
International students	5	1.6	5	1.5	0.1	
Percentages larger for private institutions						
All first-year students are required to take it	147	47.0	292	86.9	-39.9	***

Note. If *All first-year students are required to take it* was selected, respondents could not select other responses. Additionally, institutions indicating that no students were required to take a first-year seminar were not able to respond to this question due to the skip logic of the online questionnaire.

[a]Analysis was not conducted due to cell counts less than five.

$^{**}p < .01$. $^{***}p < .001$.

Sections for Unique Student Subpopulations

In addition to requiring specific populations to take the seminar, many institutions design sections for particular populations to serve their unique needs. The NSFYS asked institutions to identify unique subpopulations of students for which special sections of the first-year seminar are offered. The five most frequently identified student groups for which special sections are offered across all respondents were (a) honors students (24.1%), (b) learning community participants (19.0%), (c) academically underprepared students (16.7%), (d) students within specific majors (14.2%), and (e) undeclared students (9.2%). In addition, another 10.8% of institutions reported that special sections were offered for particular racial and ethnic groups (multiple institutions named African American males and Latino/a students specifically), summer bridge program participants, veterans, students with disabilities, and students in leadership programs.

When these results are broken down by institutional type, four-year institutions offer specific sections for the following student groups at a significantly higher rate than two-year institutions ($p < .05$ or lower): honors, undeclared, specific majors, preprofessional, transfer, and international students (Table 5). Yet, two-year colleges identified special sections for students taking developmental or remedial coursework and those in dual-enrollment programs more often than their four-year counterparts. Further, two-year institutions were more likely to report not offering any special sections of the seminar.

Public institutions were significantly more likely to provide special sections for a wide variety of student types ($p < .01$), including learning community participants, students in specific majors, student athletes, TRIO participants, students in developmental courses, undeclared students, and preprofessional students (Table 6). Private institutions were significantly more likely to report that they did not offer special sections for specific populations ($p < .05$).

Table 5

Special Sections of First-Year Seminars Offered to Unique Student Subpopulations by Institutional Type ($n = 780$)

	Institutional type					
	Two-year		Four-year			
Catergory of student	**Freq.**	**%**	**Freq.**	**%**	**Difference (%)**	***p***
Percentages larger for two-year institutions						
No special sections are offered	92	46.5	213	36.6	9.9	*
Students enrolled in developmental or remedial courses	22	11.1	24	4.1	7.0	***
Students participating in dual-enrollment programs	6	3.0	6	1.0	2.0	*
Academically underprepared students	35	17.7	95	16.3	1.4	
Other	23	11.6	61	10.5	1.1	
Percentages larger for four-year institutions						
Honors students	7	3.5	181	31.1	-27.6	***
Undeclared students	5	2.5	67	11.5	-9.0	***
Students within specific majors	18	9.1	93	16.0	-6.9	*
Preprofessional students	5	2.5	55	9.5	-6.9	**
Provisionally admitted students	0	0.0	38	6.5	-6.5	a
Transfer students	6	3.0	52	8.9	-5.9	**
Students residing within a particular residence hall	0	0.0	29	5.0	-5.0	a
International students	7	3.5	47	8.1	-4.5	*
Learning community participants	33	16.7	115	19.8	-3.1	
First-generation students	6	3.0	35	6.0	-3.0	
TRIO participants	9	4.5	35	6.0	-1.5	
Student athletes	15	7.6	45	7.7	-0.2	

[a]Analysis was not conducted due to cell counts less than 5.

*$p < .05$. **$p < .01$. ***$p < .001$.

Table 6
Special Sections of First-Year Seminars Offered to Unique Student Subpopulations by Institutional Control ($n = 780$)

Category of student	Institutional control					
	Public		Private			
	Freq	%	Freq.	%	Difference (%)	*p*
Percentages larger for public institutions						
Learning community participants	112	26.6	36	10.0	16.6	***
Students within specific majors	81	19.2	30	8.4	10.9	***
Other	64	15.2	20	5.6	9.6	***
Student athletes	50	11.9	10	2.8	9.1	***
TRIO participants	37	8.8	7	1.9	6.8	***
Students enrolled in developmental or remedial courses	38	9.0	8	2.2	6.8	***
Undeclared students	52	12.4	20	5.6	6.8	**
Preprofessional students	45	10.7	15	4.2	6.5	***
First-generation students	29	6.9	12	3.3	3.5	*
Students residing within a particular residence hall	22	5.2	7	1.9	3.3	*
Academically underprepared students	75	17.8	55	15.3	2.5	
Provisionally admitted students	25	5.9	13	3.6	2.3	
Students participating in dual-enrollment programs	10	2.4	2	0.6	1.8	[a]
International students	32	7.6	22	6.1	1.5	
Percentages larger for private institutions						
No special sections are offered	148	35.2	157	43.7	-8.6	*
Honors students	91	21.6	97	27.0	-5.4	
Transfer students	30	7.1	28	7.8	-0.7	

[a]Analysis was not conducted due to cell counts less than five.
*$p < .05$. **$p < .01$. ***$p < .001$.

Course Characteristics

To gather a picture of the structural features of the first-year seminar, the NSFYS asked respondents to provide information about characteristics of the course. Results related to class size of each section of the seminar, awarding and application of academic credit, and the number of classroom contact hours are presented below. While not presenting a comprehensive picture of the features of the course, these areas provide a broad understanding of how first-year seminars are configured on campuses across the United States.

Seminar Class Size

Institutions were asked to provide information about the approximate class size for each section of the first-year seminar. Response options for this question included six categories representing a range of students per section. However, the analyses presented in this report used a dichotomous measure of class size: classes with 19 or fewer students or classes with 20 or more students. This break point for class size is a marker frequently found in practice and college rankings (Morse & Flanigan, 2012; Padgett & Keup, 2011). Slightly more than half of the institutions (55.6%) reported class sizes of 20 or more students.

Disaggregating the responses revealed a larger proportion of responding campuses with 20 or more students in the classroom at two-year colleges, public institutions, and campuses with a first-year class over 1,001 students (Figure 10). Additionally, the analysis revealed a larger proportion with 19 or fewer students in each section at private institutions and on campuses with incoming first-year classes of less than 500 students. Finally, four-year institutions and campuses with 501-1,000 incoming first-year students reported sections with fewer than 19 students at the same rate as sections with 20 or more. As might be expected, there is a positive relationship between entering first-year class size and proportion of sections with 20 students or more.

Figure 11 presents the number of students in each section broken down by first-year seminar type. Institutions with academic seminars on various topics comprised the only group where the majority of respondents indicated 19 or fewer students were enrolled in each section. Not only did more institutions with this type of course report smaller class sizes, they did so at nearly twice the rate as campuses reporting 20 or more students per section. Conversely, institutions with extended orientation, preprofessional or discipline-linked, and basic study skills seminars as the primary seminar type reported sections with 20 or more students at nearly twice the rate as colleges and universities with fewer students enrolled in each section.

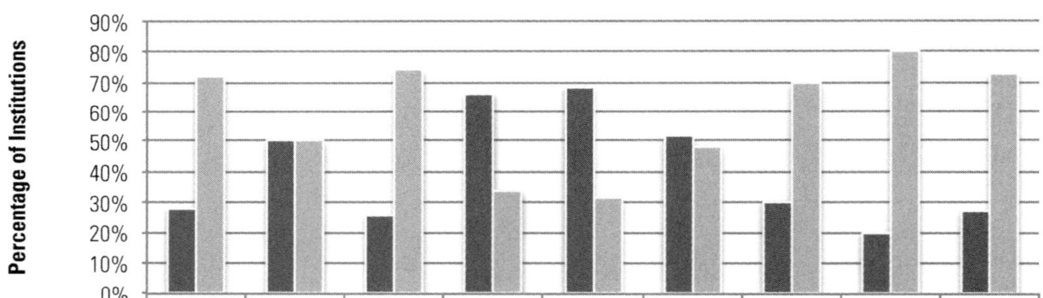

	Institution Type		Institution Control		Number of Entering First-Year Students				
	Two-year	Four-year	Public	Private	Less than 500	501 - 1,000	1,001 - 2,000	2,001 - 4,000	More than 4,000
19 or fewer	28.1%	50.0%	25.9%	66.3%	68.5%	51.7%	30.5%	19.7%	27.2%
20 or more	71.9%	50.0%	74.1%	33.7%	31.5%	48.3%	69.5%	80.3%	72.8%

Institutional Characteristics

Figure 10. Number of students per section of the seminar by institutional characteristics ($n = 783$).
$p < .001$.

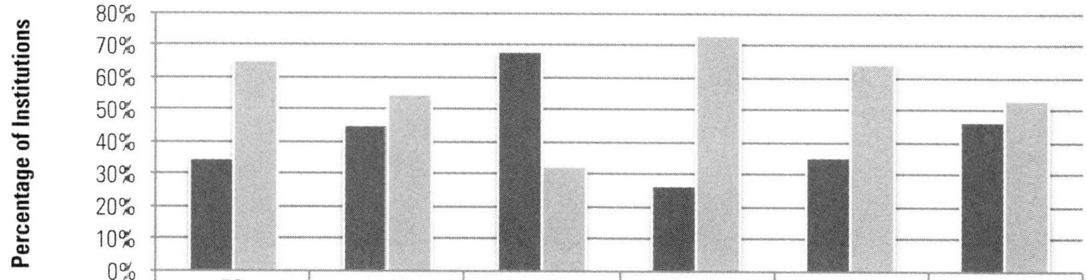

	EO	A-UC	A-VT	PP-D	BSS	HY
19 or fewer	35.0%	45.0%	67.8%	26.7%	35.5%	46.8%
20 or more	65.0%	55.0%	32.2%	73.3%	64.5%	53.2%

Primary Seminar Type

Figure 11. Number of students per section by primary seminar type ($n = 783$). EO = extended orientation, A-UC = academic – uniform content, A-VT = academic – various topics, PP-D = preprofessional or discipline-linked, BSS = basic study skills, HY = hybrid.
$p < .001$.

Academic Credit

Nearly all institutions (94.5%) reported that the first-year seminar on their campus carries academic credit. When broken down by institutional characteristics such as type, control, and the number of entering first-year students and by primary seminar type, there was no significant difference in the frequency of institutions offering the seminar for credit.

However, credit offered for the seminar is not assigned in the same way across institutions. As illustrated in Figure 12, the majority of campuses applied first-year seminar credits toward general education requirements (58.6%), followed by 37.9% of the institutions applying it as an elective. Only 8.5% of institutions reported applying the credit toward major requirements.

This distribution was magnified across four-year and private institutions (Figure 12); however, at two-year and public campuses, the first-year seminar credit was more frequently applied as an elective. Figure 13 illustrates a positive relationship between the percentage of institutions that applied the seminar credit as an elective and the number of entering first-year students. Alternatively, there was a negative relationship in the proportion of institutions that applied the seminar toward general education credits and entering first-year class size. The point where these two trends appear to cross is in institutions with 2,001-4,000 first-year students. That is to say, institutions with 2,000 or fewer students in their first-year cohort reported applying seminar credit toward general education requirements, while campuses with more than 4,000 students reported applying seminar credit as an elective. Colleges and universities at that crossing point reported application of seminar credit as an elective (50.0%) or a general education requirement (46.6%) at nearly equal rates.

When the application of seminar credit is disaggregated by primary seminar type, patterns of note emerge, as seen in Figure 14. Institutions with preprofessional and basic study skills as a primary seminar type report applying credit as an elective more frequently than institutions where other types are more prevalent. Credit applied toward general education requirements is predominant in institutions with hybrid and academic seminars of either type. Institutions with an extended orientation as a primary first-year seminar report application of seminar credit as an elective and toward general education requirements at approximately the same rate. In other words, credit for academically focused and hybrid seminars was more likely to be applied toward general education requirements, while preprofessional or discipline-linked and basic study skills seminars were more likely counted as electives. Credit for extended orientation seminars was applied as elective or general education requirements at equal rates.

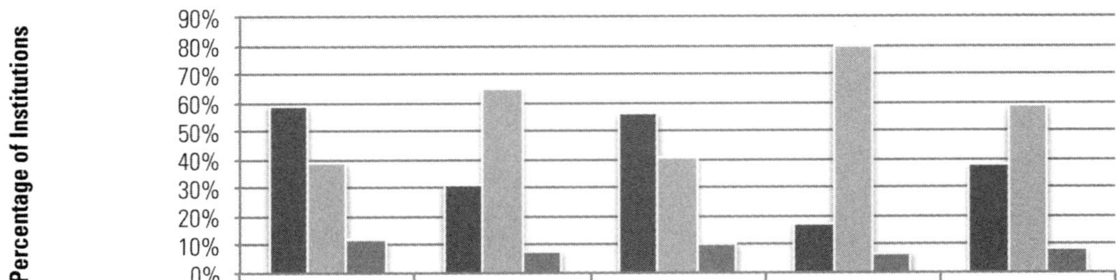

	Institution Type		Institution Control		
	Two-year	Four-year	Public	Private	Total
■ Elective	59.1%	31.1%	56.0%	17.1%	37.92%
■ General education	38.6%	65.1%	40.7%	79.3%	58.61%
■ Major requirements	11.4%	7.5%	10.1%	6.6%	8.47%

Institutional Characteristics

Figure 12. Application of first-year seminar credit by institutional type and control ($n = 720$). The sum of the column percentages may be larger than 100% due to the ability of respondents to select more than one response.
$p < .001$.

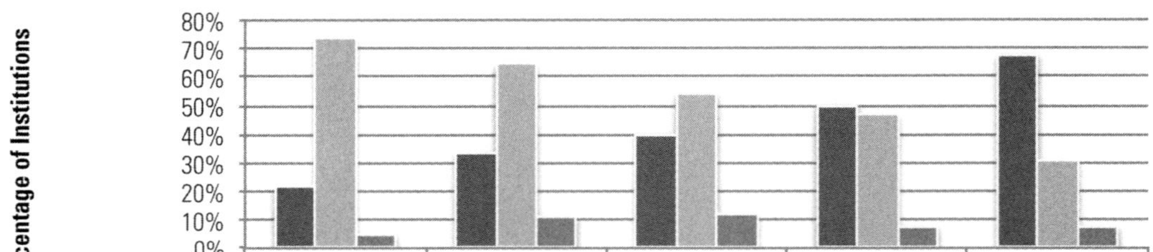

	Number of Entering First-Year Students				
	Less than 500	501 - 1,000	1,001 - 2,000	2,001 - 4,000	More than 4,000
■ Elective	21.6%	33.7%	40.1%	50.0%	67.9%
■ General education	74.2%	64.5%	54.2%	46.6%	30.9%
■ Major requirements	5.2%	10.8%	12.0%	7.6%	7.4%

Institutional Characteristics

Figure 13. Application of first-year seminar credit by size of entering first-year class ($n = 720$). The sum of the column percentages may be larger than 100% due to the ability of respondents to select more than one response.
$p < .001$.

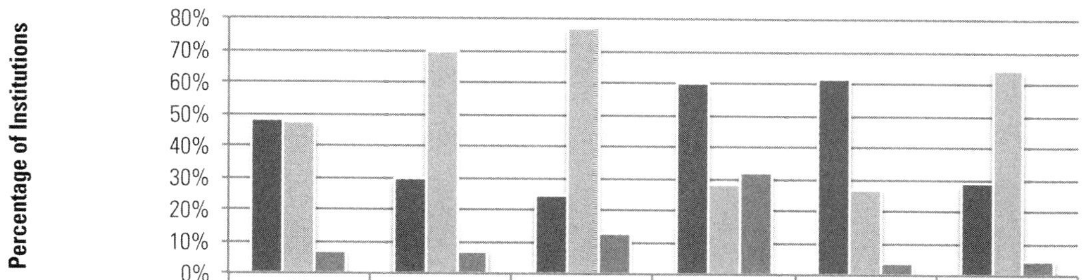

	EO	A-UC	A-VT	PP-D	BSS	HY
Elective	48.5%	29.6%	24.3%	60.0%	61.5%	28.8%
General education	47.1%	69.7%	77.1%	28.0%	26.9%	64.4%
Major requirements	6.9%	7.0%	12.5%	32.0%	3.8%	4.8%

Primary Seminar Type

Figure 14. Application of first-year seminar credit by primary seminar type ($n = 720$). The sum of the column percentages may be larger than 100% due to the ability of respondents to select more than one response. EO = extended orientation, A-UC = academic – uniform content, A-VT = academic – various topics, PP-D = preprofessional or discipline-linked, BSS = basic study skills, HY = hybrid.
$p < .001$.

The comparisons of the frequency of the use of seminar credit as an elective and a general education requirement across type, control, number of first-year students, and primary seminar type are all statistically significant at $p < .001$. While there is some variability in the application of first-year seminar credit toward major requirements by type, control, and number of entering first-year students, none of these differences rose to the level of statistical significance. Institutions with a preprofessional or discipline-linked seminar as their primary type reported applying seminar credit toward major requirements at a much higher rate (32.0%) than all other types (range of 3.9%-12.5%); however, an analysis of the application of credit toward major requirements by primary first-year seminar type was not conducted due to small numbers of responses in the cross-categories.

Classroom Contact Hours

Three in 10 responding institutions report that the course consists of one contact hour per week. An additional 22.3% hold class for two hours each week. Thus, a combined 52.3% of institutions indicated the seminar meets for two or fewer hours per week. Another 38.4% of campuses reported the course met for three hours each week. Institutional characteristics, such as control, type, or size of first-year class, were not related to an increased number of contact hours per week in first-year seminars in a statistically significant way. Notwithstanding, the number of contact hours in the course differed by the primary seminar type ($p < .001$). The distributions of contact hours by primary seminar types are presented in Figure 15. Academic seminars on various topics had more classroom contact hours per week than all other seminar types. Additionally, basic study skills, hybrid, and academic seminars with uniform content were all associated with more classroom contact hours than extended orientation and preprofessional or discipline-linked seminars.

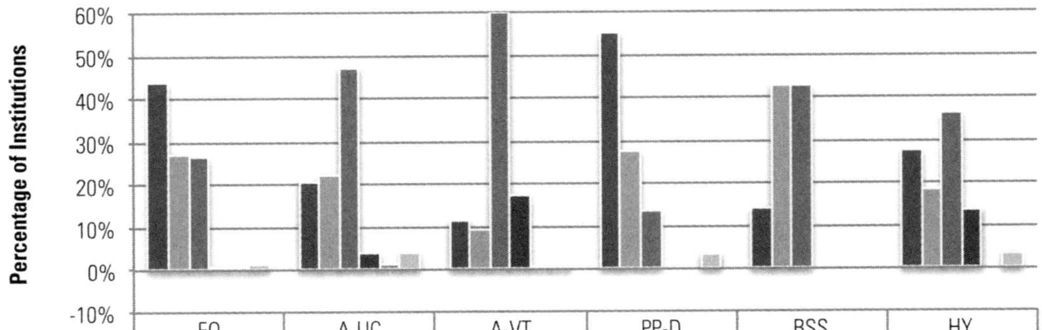

	EO	A-UC	A-VT	PP-D	BSS	HY
1 hour	43.6%	20.9%	11.6%	55.2%	14.3%	27.8%
2 hours	27.4%	22.3%	9.5%	27.6%	42.9%	18.5%
3 hours	26.4%	47.3%	59.9%	13.8%	42.9%	36.1%
4 hours	1.0%	4.1%	17.7%	0.0%	0.0%	13.9%
5 hours	0.3%	1.4%	0.7%	0.0%	0.0%	0.0%
> 6 hours	1.4%	4.1%	0.7%	3.4%	0.0%	3.7%

Primary Seminar Type

Figure 15. Total classroom contact hours per week by primary seminar type ($n = 763$). The sum of the column percentages may be larger than 100% due to the ability of respondents to select more than one response. EO = extended orientation, A-UC = academic – uniform content, A-VT = academic – various topics, PP-D = preprofessional or discipline-linked, BSS = basic study skills, HY = hybrid.
$p < .001$.

Course Content: Objectives and Topics

To better understand the content being delivered in first-year seminars nationwide, the NSFYS asked responding institutions to identify the three most important course objectives and the three most important topics covered in the seminar. These two areas are helpful in understanding institutional strategic goals for the seminar and the content of the course. Moreover, it can provide insight into whether course content is aligned to achieve course goals.

Course Objectives

Overall, the three most frequent course objectives identified for the first-year seminar were to (a) develop a connection with the institution (44.9%), (b) provide orientation to campus resources and services (37.8%), and (c) develop academic skills (36.3%). These objectives are consistent with the historical role of the first-year seminar and are the same top three objectives identified in the 2009 administration of the survey (Padgett & Keup, 2011). Further, 8.1% of responding institutions reported other objectives. The most prevalent of these other objectives were developing research skills, setting personal and professional goals, engaging students with "big questions," and fostering ethical reasoning skills. Several faith-based colleges and universities described objectives aimed at integrating learning and the religious tradition of the institution.

Table 7 provides a breakdown of course objectives by institutional type. Two-year colleges were significantly more likely to report using the seminar to develop study skills, to provide opportunities for self-exploration or personal development, to provide career exploration, and to provide an orientation to campus resources and services ($p < .05$ or lower). Taken collectively, the objectives more prevalent in community colleges focus on refining college success skills and personal development.

The objectives identified by four-year institutions at significantly higher levels ($p < .05$ or lower) include developing writing skills, enhancing critical-thinking skills, introducing the liberal arts, increasing student-faculty interaction, and creating a common first-year experience. These objectives suggest a focus on intellectual skill development and fostering a sense of belonging on campus.

Table 7

Course Objectives for First-Year Seminars by Institutional Type ($n = 761$)

Catergory of student	Institutional type: Two-year Freq.	Two-year %	Four-year Freq.	Four-year %	Difference (%)	p
Percentages larger for two-year institutions						
Develop study skills	84	44.7	68	11.9	32.8	***
Provide orientation to campus resources and services	90	47.9	198	34.6	13.3	**
Self-exploration or personal development	50	26.6	79	13.8	12.8	***
Provide career exploration	24	12.8	24	4.2	8.6	***
Develop financial literacy	8	4.3	4	0.7	3.6	a
Develop academic skills	71	37.8	205	35.8	2.0	
Develop intercultural competence	2	1.1	4	0.7	0.4	a
Percentages larger for four-year institutions						
Develop writing skills	1	0.5	87	15.2	-14.7	a
Develop critical-thinking skills	27	14.4	150	26.2	-11.3	***
Introduce the liberal arts	1	0.5	62	10.8	-10.3	a
Increase student-faculty interaction	11	5.9	83	14.5	-8.6	**
Create common first-year experience	30	16.0	134	23.4	-7.4	*
Introduce a discipline	3	1.6	35	6.1	-4.5	a
Develop oral communication skills	2	1.1	31	5.4	-4.3	a
Develop support network or friendships	23	12.2	87	15.2	-2.9	
Develop information literacy	11	5.9	45	7.9	-2.0	
Provide preprofessional preparation	1	0.5	14	2.4	-1.9	a
Other	13	6.9	49	8.6	-1.6	
Improve second-year return rates	26	13.8	84	14.7	-0.8	
Develop a connection with the institution	84	44.7	258	45.0	-0.3	

[a]Analysis was not conducted due to cell counts less than five.

*$p < .05$. **$p < .01$. ***$p < .001$.

Disaggregating the course objectives by institutional control, revealed that public institutions placed greater emphasis on college success skills, including navigation of campus environments and personal development in the first-year seminar. Public institutions reported study skills, academic skills, orientation to campus resources, connection to institution, and career exploration at significantly higher rates than private institutions ($p < .05$ or lower). Private institutions focused the first-year seminar on objectives such as developing writing, oral communication, and critical-thinking skills as well as creating a common first-year experience and introducing the liberal arts. Results of the frequency of course objectives broken down by institutional control are presented in Table 8.

Table 8

Course Objectives for First-Year Seminars by Institutional Control ($n = 761$)

	Institutional control					
	Public		Private			
Course objectives	Freq.	%	Freq.	%	Difference (%)	p
Percentages larger for public institutions						
Develop study skills	115	28.1	37	10.5	17.6	***
Provide orientation to campus resources and services	187	45.7	101	28.7	17.0	***
Develop academic skills	168	41.1	108	30.7	10.4	**
Develop a connection with the institution	199	48.7	143	40.6	8.0	*
Provide career exploration	37	9.0	11	3.1	5.9	***
Self-exploration or personal development	73	17.8	56	15.9	1.9	
Introduce a discipline	24	5.9	14	4.0	1.9	
Improve second-year return rates	62	15.2	48	13.6	1.5	
Develop financial literacy	9	2.2	3	0.9	1.3	a
Provide preprofessional preparation	10	2.4	5	1.4	1.0	
Develop intercultural competence	4	1.0	2	0.6	0.4	a
Increase student-faculty interaction	51	12.5	43	12.2	0.3	
Percentages larger for private institutions						
Develop writing skills	11	2.7	77	21.9	-19.2	***
Develop critical-thinking skills	72	17.6	105	29.8	-12.2	***
Create common first-year experience	67	16.4	97	27.6	-11.2	***
Introduce the liberal arts	14	3.4	49	13.9	-10.5	***
Develop oral communication skills	7	1.7	26	7.4	-5.7	***
Develop information literacy	24	5.9	32	9.1	-3.2	
Other	28	6.8	34	9.7	-2.8	
Develop support network or friendships	56	13.7	54	15.3	-1.6	

[a]Analysis was not conducted due to cell counts less than 5.

$^*p < .05$. $^{**}p < .01$. $^{***}p < .001$.

As explained earlier in this section, when taken in the aggregate, the most frequently reported course objectives in the first-year seminar were to develop a connection with the institution, provide orientation to campus resources and services, and develop academic skills. However, there were some differences in predominant course objectives based on primary seminar type (Table 9). Extended orientation and hybrid seminars most frequently reported objectives aimed at connecting students to the institution, orienting the students to campus resources, and developing academic skills. While respondents with either academically based primary seminar selected the development of academic skills as one of the important goals of the seminar, there was divergence with the other two top objectives for each seminar type. For institutions offering an academic seminar with uniform content as the primary type, the other top objectives were to create a common first-year experience and develop a connection with the institution. Alternately, those campuses with academic seminars on various topics more frequently reported critical-thinking and writing skill development as course goals. As would be expected, campuses with preprofessional or discipline-based seminars selected the introduction of a discipline and preprofessional preparation as objectives. Similarly, institutions with a basic study skills primary seminar indicated an orientation to campus services and development of academic and study skills as goals for the course.

Table 9

Most Frequently Reported Course Objectives by Primary Seminar Type (n = 761)

	Primary Seminar Type					
Course objectives	**EO**	**A-UC**	**A-VT**	**PP-D**	**BSS**	**HY**
Create common first-year experience		35.8%				
Develop a connection with the institution	56.3%	36.5%		41.4%		49.5%
Develop academic skills	34.6%	37.8%	32.0%		46.4%	45.8%
Develop critical-thinking skills			50.3%			
Develop study skills					67.9%	
Develop writing skills			38.8%			
Introduce a discipline				48.3%		
Provide orientation to campus resources and services	58.3%				50.0%	34.6%
Provide preprofessional preparation				41.4%		

Note. The three most frequent responses for each seminar type are reported; all other frequencies have been suppressed. EO = extended orientation, A-UC = academic – uniform content, A-VT = academic – various topics, PP-D = preprofessional or discipline-linked, BSS = basic study skills, HY = hybrid.

Course Topics

Where course objectives set the overall focus and provide a purpose for the first-year seminar, course topics are one way to achieve those goals. The most frequently reported course goals were to develop a connection with the institution, provide orientation to campus resources and services, and develop academic skills, and the topics most often identified were aligned with those goals. The top three topics reported by responding institutions were (a) campus resources (35.7%), (b) academic planning or advising (34.7%), and (c) critical thinking (32.6%). While a topic directly related to the objective of connecting the students to the institution was not present in the three most frequently reported, campus engagement (27.7%) was the fifth most frequently identified course topic. Another 13.9% of colleges and universities described other seminar topics, such as civic engagement; adjustment to the collegiate environment; responding to higher academic expectations; and personal exploration, including discovering one's strengths.

A review of the results presented in Table 10 highlights the differences in responses of institutions by type. For instance, two-year campuses were more than twice as likely ($p < .001$) to report emphasizing study skills and career exploration in the seminar. Additionally, two-year institutions reported with significantly greater frequency the inclusion of campus resources, time management, academic planning or advising, college policies and procedures, and financial literacy as topics in the seminar ($p < .05$ or lower). These topics demonstrate a greater focus in the seminars at two-year colleges on college success and life-skills development. Four-year institutions reported critical thinking, information literacy, and specific disciplinary topics with greater frequency. Additionally, four-year campuses were approximately 10 times more likely to focus on writing skills than community colleges. The topics identified by four-year campuses point to a concentration on intellectual skill development in the seminar.

When the topics presented in first-year seminars are disaggregated by institutional control, a pattern similar to institutional type emerges. As illustrated by Table 11, public institutions indicated they included study skills, campus resources, career exploration, academic planning, time management, and college policies and procedures in their seminars at significantly higher rates than responding private institutions ($p < .05$ or lower). This collection of topics is similar to those offered by two-year colleges and stresses the importance of college success skills in these institutions' seminars. Correspondingly, seminars at private institutions focused more frequently on writing skills, specific disciplinary topics, information literacy, and oral communication skills. Furthermore, private institutions were more likely to identify writing skills, relationship issues, and critical-thinking skills as topics covered in the seminar than responding public institutions. Again, these topics point to a focus on intellectual skill and personal development in seminars offered on private campuses.

The distribution of the three most frequently identified topics by primary seminar type as presented in Table 12 reveals very little consensus about topics offered across seminars. Agreement was found between campuses with hybrid and academic seminars with uniform content as primary seminars where the same three topics were reported with greatest prominence, namely campus engagement, critical thinking, and academic advising. Further, academic planning or advising was among the most frequently identified topic by institutions with extended orientation, academic with uniform content, preprofessional or discipline-linked, and hybrid primary seminar types. Beyond these, however, primary seminars most often emphasized topics specific to the type. For example, colleges and universities with preprofessional or discipline-linked seminars reported academic planning, career exploration, and specific disciplinary topics as the top three content areas. Similarly, study skills, time management, and campus resources were the topics reported by campuses with basic study skills seminars as the primary type.

Table 10
Topics for a First-Year Seminar by Institutional Type (n = 761)

Course topics	Two-year Freq.	Two-year %	Four-year Freq.	Four-year %	Difference (%)	p
Percentages larger for two-year institutions						
Study skills	95	50.5	132	23.0	27.5	***
Career exploration or preparation	55	29.3	75	13.1	16.2	***
Campus resources	90	47.9	182	31.8	16.1	***
Time management	63	33.5	109	19.0	14.5	***
Academic planning or advising	84	44.7	180	31.4	13.3	***
College policies and procedures	31	16.5	63	11.0	5.5	*
Financial literacy	10	5.3	8	1.4	3.9	**
Relationship issues	16	8.5	42	7.3	1.2	
Percentages larger for four-year institutions						
Writing skills	4	2.1	128	22.3	-20.2	a
Critical thinking	33	17.6	215	37.5	-20.0	***
Specific disciplinary topic	5	2.7	95	16.6	-13.9	***
Other	13	6.9	93	16.2	-9.3	**
Campus engagement	42	22.3	169	29.5	-7.2	
Oral communication skills	1	0.5	38	6.6	-6.1	a
Information literacy	11	5.9	66	11.5	-5.7	*
Global learning	0	0.0	25	4.4	-4.4	a
Diversity issues	7	3.7	29	5.1	-1.3	
Health and wellness	1	0.5	10	1.7	-1.2	a

[a]Analysis was not conducted due to cell counts less than five.
$*p < .05$. $**p < .01$. $***p < .001$.

Table 11

Topics for a First-Year Seminar by Institutional Control ($n = 761$)

	Institutional control					
	Public		Private			
Course topics	**Freq.**	**%**	**Freq.**	**%**	**Difference (%)**	***p***
Percentages larger for public						
Study skills	173	42.3	54	15.3	27.0	***
Campus resources	186	45.5	86	24.4	21.0	***
Career exploration or preparation	95	23.2	35	9.9	13.3	***
Academic planning or advising	164	40.1	100	28.4	11.7	***
Time management	113	27.6	59	16.8	10.9	***
College policies and procedures	62	15.2	32	9.1	6.1	*
Financial literacy	13	3.2	5	1.4	1.8	
Diversity issues	20	4.9	16	4.5	0.3	
Percentages larger for private						
Critical thinking	91	22.2	157	44.6	-22.4	***
Writing skills	30	7.3	102	29.0	-21.6	***
Other	38	9.3	68	19.3	-10.0	***
Specific disciplinary topic	42	10.3	58	16.5	-6.2	**
Information literacy	31	7.6	46	13.1	-5.5	*
Relationship issues	21	5.1	37	10.5	-5.4	**
Oral communication skills	11	2.7	28	8.0	-5.3	**
Campus engagement	104	25.4	107	30.4	-5.0	
Global learning	11	2.7	14	4.0	-1.3	
Health and wellness	5	1.2	6	1.7	-0.5	

*$p < .05$. **$p < .01$. ***$p < .001$.

Table 12

Most Frequently Reported Topics for a First-Year Seminar by Primary Seminar Type (n = 761)

	Primary seminar type					
Course topics	**EO**	**A-UC**	**A-VT**	**PP-D**	**BSS**	**HY**
Academic planning or advising	47.1%	35.1%		41.4%		31.8%
Career exploration or preparation				44.8%		
Campus engagement		27.7%				34.6%
Campus resources	56.3%				46.4%	
Critical thinking		45.9%	63.3%			37.4%
Specific disciplinary topic			33.3%	44.8%		
Study skills	39.3%				67.9%	
Time management					42.9%	
Writing skills			49.0%			

Note. The three most frequent responses for each seminar type are reported; all other frequencies have been suppressed. EO = extended orientation, A-UC = academic – uniform content, A-VT = academic – various topics, PP-D = preprofessional or discipline-linked, BSS = basic study skills, HY = hybrid.

These results suggest that overall, the course content in the first-year seminar represented by course objectives and topics is largely aligned. Efforts in the seminar appear to be aimed at assisting students to develop a connection with the institution, providing orientation to campus resources and services, and developing academic skills. These emphases are consistent with theory, particularly developing a connection to the institution (Hurtado & Carter, 1997; Tinto, 1993), and best practices in the first-year seminar (Hunter & Linder, 2005).

Teaching the First-Year Seminar

The final characteristic of the first-year seminar this report will highlight is instruction. This section focuses on two questions regarding instruction of the first-year seminars: (a) *Who teaches the first-year seminar?* and (b) *If undergraduates assist in the first-year seminar, what is their primary role?*

Instructor of the Seminar

The NSFYS asked institutions to identify the professional role of the individual charged with teaching the first-year seminar. The response options for this question included three categories of instructors: (a) faculty, (b) staff, and (c) students. Respondents were allowed to identify one or more instructor for the seminar. As such, faculty were cited most frequently as the group teaching the first-year seminar. Individually, institutions named tenure-track (71.1%), full-time non-tenure-track (60.7%), or adjunct (51.9%) faculty as instructors of the course. When all faculty roles are combined, 80.5% of all institutions identified at least one of the three types of faculty as the instructor of the seminar. Additionally, 54.7% of campuses reported the seminar was taught by a staff member, either a student affairs professional (52.0%) or another campus professional (31.8%). Graduate students were mentioned as instructors by only 4.8% of institutions, and undergraduates were reported at the rate of 4.1%.

When responses were grouped by institutional type, two-year institutions reported significantly more adjunct faculty ($p < .001$) teaching the first-year seminar (Table 13). No two-year colleges reported undergraduate students as the instructor of the seminar. Similarly, all institutions identifying graduate students as the instructors of the seminar were four-year campuses. This result is to be expected as two-year campuses lack the graduate programs from which these instructors could be drawn. Significantly more four-year institutions reported tenure-track and full-time non-tenure-track faculty as well as other campus professionals as instructors in the first-year seminar ($p < .05$ or lower).

Table 13

Professional Role of First-Year Seminar Instructor by Institutional Type ($n = 779$)

	Institutional type					
	Two-year		Four-year			
Instructor role	Freq.	%	Freq.	%	Difference (%)	*p*
Percentage higher for two-year institutions						
Adjunct faculty	145	73.2	259	44.5	28.7	***
Student affairs professionals	111	56.1	294	50.5	5.5	
Percentage higher for four-year institutions						
Tenure-track faculty	104	52.5	450	77.3	-24.8	***
Other campus professionals	39	19.7	209	35.9	-16.2	***
Full-time non-tenure-track faculty	107	54.0	366	62.9	-8.8	*
Graduate students	0	0.0	37	6.4	-6.4	a
Undergraduate students	0	0.0	32	5.5	-5.5	a

[a]Analysis was not conducted due to cell counts less than five.
$^{*}p < .05$. $^{***}p < .001$.

Table 14 presents the prevalence of the professional role of the instructor by institutional control. Public institutions report having adjunct faculty and student affairs staff teach the seminar more frequently; they also use graduate students as instructors at a rate four times that of private institutions ($p < .001$). Furthermore, tenure-track faculty were identified as seminar instructors more frequently at private institutions than at publics. While the differences in prevalence between student affairs staff and faculty rise to the level of statistical significance based on institutional type and control, a majority of institutiotns reported using both of these groups as instructors of the first-year seminar.

Table 14

Professional Role of First-Year Seminar Instructor by Institutional Control ($n = 779$)

Instructor role	Institutional control				Difference (%)	*p*
	Public		Private			
	Freq.	%	Freq.	%		
Percentage higher for public institutions						
Adjunct faculty	259	61.7	145	40.4	21.3	***
Student affairs professionals	241	57.4	164	45.7	11.7	**
Graduate students	31	7.4	6	1.7	5.7	***
Percentage higher for private institutions						
Tenure-track faculty	281	66.9	273	76.0	-9.1	**
Full-time non-tenure-track faculty	246	58.6	227	63.2	-4.7	
Other campus professionals	129	30.7	119	33.1	-2.4	
Undergraduate students	16	3.8	16	4.5	-0.6	

**$p < .01$. ***$p < .001$.

Using the institution's primary seminar type to group responses to the question of who teaches the seminar revealed similarities across types. The most frequently identified instructor for each seminar type is listed below:

- extended orientation: student affairs professional (70.7%),
- academic seminar – uniform content: tenure-track faculty (67.6%),
- academic seminar – various topics: tenure-track faculty (91.2%),
- preprofessional or discipline-linked: tenure-track faculty (83.3%),
- basic study skills: adjunct faculty (87.1%), and
- hybrid: tenure-track faculty (77.5%).

These results show that despite the primary seminar type, institutions rely on faculty, tenure-track in most cases, to teach the seminar. Campuses with basic study skills courses were alone in their identification of adjunct faculty as the predominant professional role of instructors. The extended orientation seminar was the only type in which a majority of respondents did not identify faculty as course instructors; student affairs professionals were the most frequently named instructors of that type of course.

Role of Undergraduate Students in the Seminar

Since 1991, administrations of the NSFYS have asked about the use of undergraduate students to teach the first-year seminar. The survey questionnaire has asked institutions to respond to two items about undergraduate roles in the seminar: (a) if undergraduates are instructors of the first-year seminar and (b) the roles undergraduates play if they assist in the seminar. The proportion of institutions that identified students as the instructors in all prior surveys varied between 5.1% (2009 administration; Padgett & Keup, 2011) and 10.0% (2000 administration; National Resource Center, 2002). Reports for administrations prior to 2009 did not report the responses to the question asking institutions to identify the roles undergraduates play in the seminar (National Resource Center, 2002; Tobolowsky, 2005; Tobolowsky & Associates, 2008). Moreover, in the 2009 administration, the branching pattern of the survey permitted only those institutions that indicated undergraduates were instructors of the course to respond to the follow-up question about roles of these students in the first-year seminar. As a result, the best estimate for the prevalence of institutions using undergraduates in the first-year seminar relied on the responses to the question on whether these students were instructors (i.e., 5%-10%). The 2012-2013 administration changed that branching pattern to permit all institutions to report on the roles of undergraduate students in the seminar, irrespective of their status as instructors of the course.

More than 10 times as many institutions (46.3%) reported that undergraduates played a role in the first-year seminar as those indicating these students taught the course (4.1%). However, the use of peers in the seminar was not consistent across institutional characteristics. For example, nearly 9 out of 10 two-year institutions (88.4%) reported they do not use undergraduate peer leaders in any way in the first-year seminar (Table 15). In contrast, more four-year institutions (57.8%) used undergraduates in the first-year seminar, whether as assistants or co-instructors. Four-year institutions also reported that undergraduates teach independently more frequently than two-year colleges; however, the numbers of responses were so few for both types of institutions that caution should be exercised when interpreting this result.

Table 15

Role of Undergraduate Students Who Assist in First-Year Seminars by Institutional Type ($n = 764$)

	Institutional type					
	Two-year		Four-year			
Primary undergraduate role	Freq.	%	Freq.	%	Difference (%)	*p*
Percentage higher for two-year institutions						
Undergraduate students do not assist in the seminar	168	88.4	242	42.2	46.3	***
Percentage higher for four-year institutions						
They assist the instructor, but do not teach	12	6.3	195	34.0	-27.7	***
Other	8	4.2	106	18.5	-14.3	***
They teach as a part of a team	5	2.6	90	15.7	-13.0	***
They teach independently	1	0.5	16	2.8	-2.3	a

[a]Analysis was not conducted due to cell counts less than five.

***$p < .001$.

Significantly more public institutions (63.3%, $p < .001$) indicated that undergraduate students do not assist in the first-year seminar (Table 16). More private institutions reported using undergraduate peer leaders to assist the instructor in a nonteaching role. While there were differences in the reported frequencies of the roles of undergraduate students when disaggregated by primary seminar, none of the differences in the distributions of responses by type were statistically significant.

Table 16

Role of Undergraduate Students Who Assist in First-Year Seminars by Institutional Control (n = 764)

	Institutional control					
	Public		Private			
Primary undergraduate role	Freq.	%	Freq.	%	Difference (%)	*p*
Percentage higher for public institutions						
Undergraduate students do not assist in the seminar	261	63.3	149	42.3	21.0	***
They teach independently	13	3.2	4	1.1	2.0	a
Percentage higher for private institutions						
They assist the instructor, but do not teach	83	20.1	124	35.2	-15.1	***
Other	52	12.6	62	17.6	-5.0	
They teach as a part of a team	46	11.2	49	13.9	-2.8	

[a]Analysis was not conducted due to cell counts less than five.

***$p < .001$.

Conclusion

The first-year seminar continues to be an important initiative to support students making the transition to higher education across the United States. Nearly 90% of responding campuses report offering a first-year seminar. Furthermore, institutions of all types are dedicating valuable resources to ensure this is a quality educational experience for students. This is evidenced by the fact that more than 80% of institutions reported faculty teach in the seminar, including over 70% that identified tenure-track faculty as instructors.

Extended orientation continues to be the predominant seminar type, both in terms of the overall number of institutions offering that type of seminar and the number of institutions reporting it as the seminar type with the highest number of students enrolled. However, academic seminars, both uniform and variable content, taken together now represent essentially the same proportion. The increase in the proportion of academic seminars and the decrease in extended orientation seminars have been steady over the 25-year history of the National Survey of First-Year Seminars (Padgett & Keup, 2011; Tobolowsky & Associates, 2008). If this trend continues, the next administration of the NSFYS will mark the first time that institutions will identify academic seminars as the predominant type.

While seminars emphasize different content across the primary types, they share a set of common goals. Institutions are making efforts for students to develop a connection with the institution, to provide orientation to campus resources and services, and to develop academic skills. The seminar is an important tool for assisting students who are not college ready, particularly at two-year and public institutions.

High-Impact Educational Practices in the First-Year Seminar

In 2007, the Association of American Colleges and Universities (AAC&U) issued a call to the U.S. higher education community for a commitment to "advance a contemporary set of goals, guiding principles, and practices that will prepare all college students ... for twenty-first-century realities" (p. 5). As part of that charge, AAC&U identified a list of 10 established educational innovations with demonstrated effectiveness with college students. The research on these "effective educational practices" (AAC&U, 2007, p. 5) shows that student participation in them leads to important outcomes, such as gains in deep learning, first-year GPA, and first- to second-year retention (Kuh, 2008), as well as, gains in 21st century learning outcomes identified through AAC&U's LEAP initiative, including integrative and applied learning, inquiry and analysis, global learning, and civic knowledge and engagement (Kuh, 2008; Leskes & Miller, 2006). Moreover, the gains are particularly significant for those students from historically underserved backgrounds (AAC&U, 2007; Kuh, 2008).

These practices, later dubbed "high-impact educational practices" (Kuh, 2008) or simply high-impact practices (HIPs), include the following curricular and cocurricular activities:

- first-year seminars and experiences,
- common intellectual experiences,
- learning communities,
- writing-intensive courses,
- collaborative assignments and projects,
- undergraduate research,
- diversity or global learning,
- service-learning or community-based learning,
- internships, and
- capstone courses and projects.

It is worth noting that first-year seminars, the focus of the National Survey of First-Year Seminars (NSFYS), were identified as a HIP. Moreover, previous administrations of the NSFYS had been asking questions about the inclusion or connection of other HIPs to the first-year seminar (Padgett & Keup, 2011; & Tobolowsky & Associates, 2008). Specifically, the survey has been gathering information on the use of learning communities, service-learning, writing practices, and common reading experiences (as common intellectual experiences).

The inclusion of questions around these activities in the NSFYS is due to the recognition that the first-year seminar frequently serves as a "curricular anchor for other first-year initiatives" (Greenfield et al., 2013, p. xxxv). Through the Documenting Effective Educational Practice (DEEP) project, Kuh, Kinzie, Schuh, and Witt (2005) identified first-year seminars at several schools as a "centerpiece of [an] effort to cultivate a supportive campus environment" (p. 113). Several of the DEEP schools offered first-year seminars that involved or were connected to curricular and cocurricular practices identified as HIPs, such as collaborative learning skills, qualitative and quantitative modes of inquiry, communities of learning, common intellectual experiences, and learning across differences.

The 2012-2013 NSFYS was designed to further investigate the role of the first-year seminar as a central situating point for HIPs in the first college year. This administration of the NSFYS explored the seminar's unifying influence during the first college year, particularly around educationally effective practices, and specifically sought evidence of intentional integration of other HIPs within the seminar, indicating a well-implemented "single multidimensional activity" (Kuh, 2010, p. xiii) and suggesting these educationally effective practices have reached their fullest potential.

To this end, the 2012-2013 administration of the NSFYS included a section on HIPs in the seminar. Institutions were asked to identify which, if any, of the following high-impact approaches were intentionally incorporated into in or connected to the seminar:

- ***Writing-intensive***—educational experiences that develop students' ability to produce and revise various forms of writing;
- ***Collaborative assignments and projects***—educational experiences that require collaboration and teamwork with other students;
- ***Diversity and global learning***—educational experiences inside or outside the classroom that help students explore cultures, life experiences, and worldviews different from their own;
- ***Service-learning***—nonremunerative service as part of a course
- ***Learning community***—linking a cohort of students in the first-year seminar to one or more other courses or to a common set of theme-based experiences
- ***Common reading experience***—first-year reading experience or summer reading program; and
- ***Undergraduate research***—scientific inquiry, creative activity, or scholarship guided by a mentor from the faculty or research staff.

Because not all of the HIPs apply to entering first-year students, the instrument excluded internships and capstone courses and projects.

The survey asked two questions related to the presence of HIPs in the seminar (Appendix B). First, among the seven HIPs listed above are initiatives based within first-year seminars. These include writing-intensive approaches, collaborative assignments, and diversity and global learning. Respondents were asked whether these initiatives were *intentionally incorporated into the first-year seminar.* Other HIPs, such as learning communities and common reading experiences, are more appropriately thought of as being linked to seminars. In other words, these practices are programs that frequently exist outside the framework of the course. Service-learning and undergraduate research may be either based in or connected to seminars. Respondents were asked to indicate whether these HIPs *are connected to the first-year seminar.* The analysis of survey responses did not distinguish between HIPs embedded in courses versus those associated with them. Thus, words and phrases such as *connected, included,* and *in conjunction* are used interchangeably throughout the discussion on HIPs in the first-year seminar to avoid repetition.

This section begins with an overview of the connection of the seminar to these educationally effective activities by describing how many and which of these practices institutions offer. An analysis of the role cocurricular HIPs play in the first-year seminar at participating institutions follows.

Prevalence of HIPs in First-Year Seminars

The inclusion of HIPs in the first-year seminar was nearly universal among the sample of institutions that participated in the survey. Among the respondents, 93.3% reported offering at least one of these practices in connection with their first-year seminar. Further, 76.4% of campuses reported offering at least two, and 54.2% indicated offering three or more of these activities in connection with first-year seminar. The distribution of the number of HIPs across respondents is presented in Figure 16.

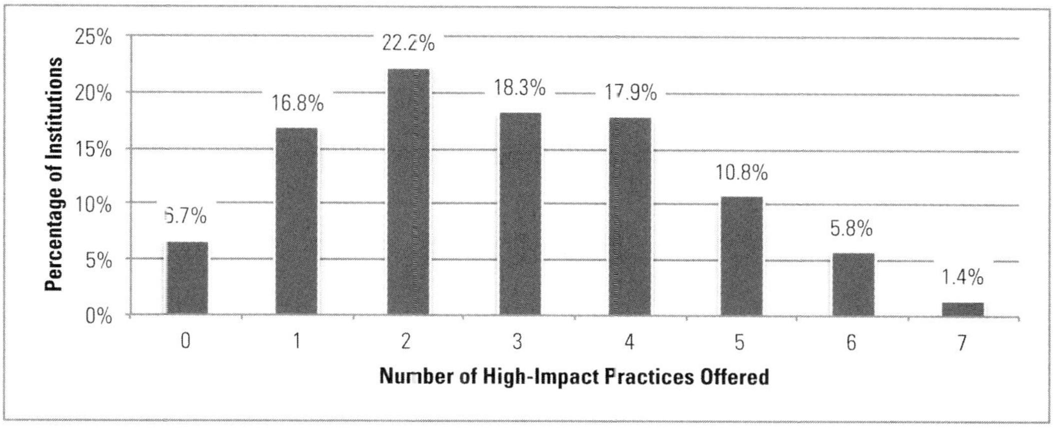

Figure 16. Total number of high-impact practices offered in conjunction with the first-year seminar (n = 760).

Table 17 presents a comparison of the average number of HIPs broken down by institutional type and control. On average, four-year institutions are significantly more likely to offer one or more of these activities in connection with first-year seminar than their two-year counterparts ($p < .001$). This comparison of the distribution disaggregated by institutional type can be seen in Figure 17. While private institutions report a slightly higher average number of HIPs than public institutions, this difference did not rise to the level of significance.

Table 17
Average Number of High-Impact Practices Offered in Conjunction With the First-Year Seminar by Institutional Characteristics (n = 760)

Institutional characteristic	*M*	*SD*	*t*	*p*
All Institutions	2.87	1.69		
Type			-7.55	< .001
Two-year	2.14	1.46		
Four-year	3.10	1.69		
Control			-1.82	.069
Public	2.76	1.69		
Private	2.99	1.68		

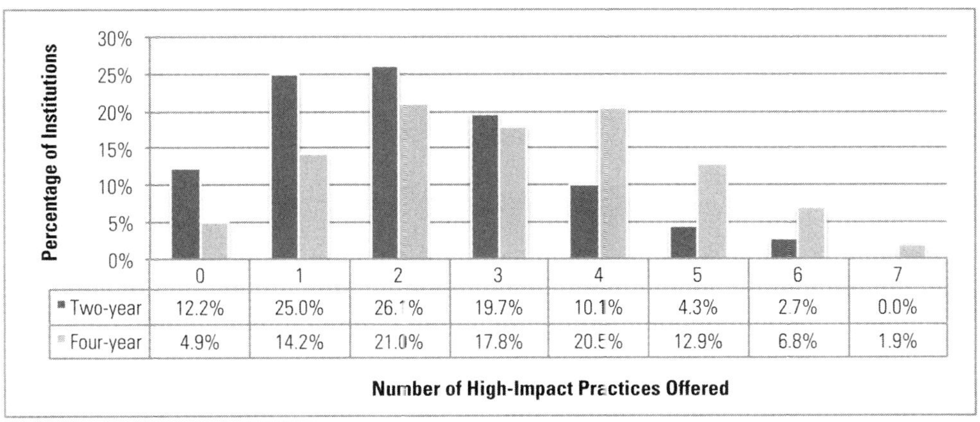

Figure 17. Total number of high-impact practices offered in conjunction with the first-year seminar by institutional type (n = 760).

There are significant differences ($p < .001$) in the number of HIPs offered in conjunction with first-year seminars when broken down by primary seminar type. Posthoc tests show that institutions with extended orientation ($M = 2.52$) as the primary first-year seminar offer significantly fewer HIPs on average than hybrid seminars ($M = 3.13$, $p < .05$), academic - uniform content ($M = 3.14$, $p < .01$), and academic - various topics ($M = 3.29$, $p < .001$). While the average number of the educationally effective practices offered at campuses with preprofessional or discipline-linked ($M = 2.55$) or basic study skills ($M = 2.29$) seminars were also lower than the campuses with hybrid and academic seminars, these differences did not rise to the level of statistical significance.

Table 18 presents the individual HIPs institutions report as connected to the first-year seminar. The three most frequently cited practices intentionally connected to the seminar were collaborative assignments and projects (67.2%), diversity and global learning (58.8%), and the inclusion of writing-intensive projects (42.5%). Notably, the most frequently cited HIPs are connected to the course curriculum and can be managed by the instructor of each section. Conversely, those cited less frequently require at least some sort of coordination beyond the confines of an individual course.

Table 18

High-Impact Educational Practices Connected to First-Year Seminars

High-impact educational practice	Freq.	%
Collaborative assignments and projects[a]	511	67.2
Diversity/global learning[a]	447	58.8
Writing-intensive[a]	323	42.5
Common reading experience[b]	286	38.1
Learning community[b]	276	36.8
Service-learning[b]	239	31.8
Undergraduate research[b]	96	12.8

Note. The NSFYS contained two separate questions on high-impact practices (see Appendix D).
[a]High-impact practices intentionally integrated into the seminar ($n = 760$)
[b]High-impact practices connected to the seminar ($n = 751$)

A disaggregation of the specific HIPs by institutional type is found in Table 19. Four-year institutions were more likely to report intentionally including five of the seven HIPs in the first-year seminar: (a) common reading experiences, (b) service-learning, (c) writing-intensive projects, (d) diversity and global learning, and (e) undergraduate research. The remaining two approaches, collaborative assignments and learning communities, were offered at roughly the same percentage of four- and two-year institutions. This is consistent with the findings presented in Table 17, and it provides insight into the specific practices that are more commonly offered on four-year campuses in the first year.

Table 19

High-Impact Educational Practices Connected to First-Year Seminars by Institutional Type

	Institutional type					
	Two-year		Four-year			
High-impact educational practice	Freq.	%	Freq.	%	Difference (%)	*p*
Percentages higher for two-year institutions						
Collaborative assignments and projects[a]	132	70.2	379	66.3	4.0	
Percentages higher for four-year institutions						
Common reading experience[b]	27	14.5	259	45.8	-31.3	***
Service-learning[b]	30	16.1	209	37.0	-20.9	***
Writing-intensive[a]	56	29.8	267	46.7	-16.9	***
Diversity or global learning[a]	88	46.8	359	62.8	-16.0	***
Undergraduate research[b]	8	4.3	88	15.6	-11.3	***
Learning community[b]	61	32.8	215	38.1	-5.3	

Note. The NSFYS contained two separate questions on high-impact practices (see Appendix D).
[a]High-impact practices intentionally integrated into the seminar ($n = 760$). [b]High-impact practices connected to the seminar ($n = 751$).
***$p < .001$.

When the specific HIPs are broken down by institutional control, private institutions were statistically more likely ($p < .001$) to report including collaborative assignments and projects and learning communities in the first-year seminar than public institutions (Table 20). Public institutions, on the other hand, were statistically more likely ($p < .001$) to report including common reading experiences, writing-intensive projects, and service-learning. The educational activities associated with undergraduate research and diversity and global learning were offered on public and private campuses at approximately the same rate.

Further investigation of the prevalence of particular HIPs based on institutional characteristics revealed that as the number of entering first-year students increased, campuses were statistically more likely to report including diversity and global learning ($p < .05$) and embedding the first-year seminar in a learning community ($p < .001$). The distributions of these results are presented in Figure 18. None of the remaining HIPs associated with the first-year seminar varied significantly based on the size of the entering first-year class.

Table 20

High-Impact Educational Practices Connected to First-Year Seminars by Institutional Control

	Institutional control					
	Public		Private			
High-impact educational practice	Freq.	%	Freq.	%	Difference (%)	p
Percentages higher for public institutions						
Collaborative assignments and projects[a]	299	73.3	212	60.2	13.1	***
Learning community[b]	172	42.5	104	30.1	12.4	***
Diversity/global learning[a]	240	58.8	207	58.8	0.0	
Percentages higher for private institutions						
Common reading experience[b]	120	29.6	166	48.0	-18.3	***
Writing-intensive[a]	145	35.5	178	50.6	-15.0	***
Service-learning[b]	106	26.2	133	38.4	-12.3	***
Undergraduate research[b]	45	11.1	51	14.7	-3.6	

Note. The NSFYS contained two separate questions on high-impact practices (see Appendix D).
[a]High-impact practices intentionally integrated into the seminar ($n = 760$). [b]High-impact practices connected to the seminar ($n = 751$).
***$p < .001$.

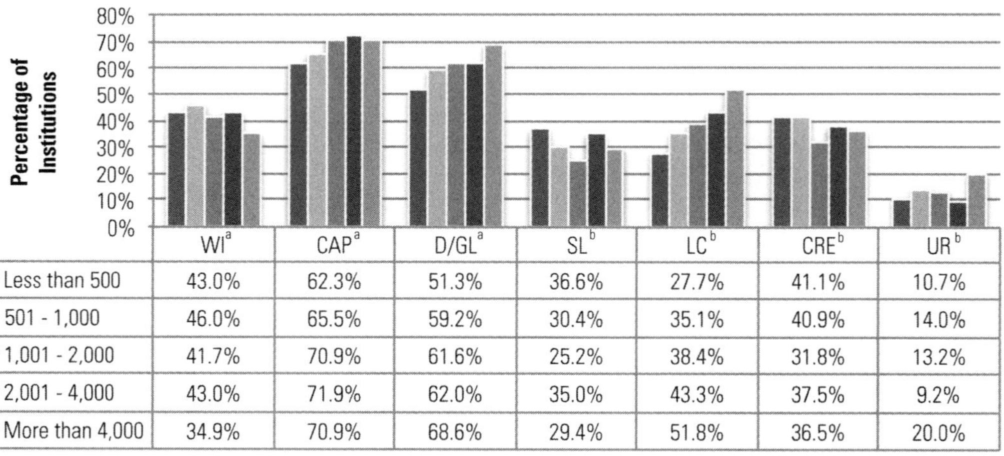

	WI[a]	CAP[a]	D/GL[a]	SL[b]	LC[b]	CRE[b]	UR[b]
Less than 500	43.0%	62.3%	51.3%	36.6%	27.7%	41.1%	10.7%
501 - 1,000	46.0%	65.5%	59.2%	30.4%	35.1%	40.9%	14.0%
1,001 - 2,000	41.7%	70.9%	61.6%	25.2%	38.4%	31.8%	13.2%
2,001 - 4,000	43.0%	71.9%	62.0%	35.0%	43.3%	37.5%	9.2%
More than 4,000	34.9%	70.9%	68.6%	29.4%	51.8%	36.5%	20.0%

High-Impact Practices

Figure 18. Percentage of institutions reporting high-impact educational practices offered in conjunction with the first-year seminar by first-year class size. WI = writing-intensive, CAP = collaborative assignments and projects, D/GL = diversity/global learning, SL = service-learning, LC = learning community, CRE = common reading experience, UR = undergraduate research. [a]High-impact practices intentionally integrated into the seminar ($n = 760$). [b]High-impact practices connected to the seminar ($n = 751$).

Structure of HIPs in First-Year Seminars

If institutions indicated they connected any of the HIPs to their first-year seminar, they were asked to provide additional information about the inclusion of the practice in the course. This section offers an overview of the information institutions provided about the cocurricular HIPs connected to the first-year seminar: (a) service-learning, (b) learning communities, (c) common reading experiences, and (d) undergraduate research. Please note that because of small cell counts (i.e., many instances of cells with less than five responses), no inferential statistics were calculated in the remaining sections for responses to the follow-up questions on HIPs. All reported differences are simply descriptive.

Service-Learning

As noted earlier, 31.8% of institutions reported offering service-learning in connection with the first-year seminar. Institutions responded to three follow-up questions drawn from responses to an open-ended question on the 2009 administration of the survey:

- *How many hours are students required to complete for the service-learning component?*
- *Which of the following are used as reflection techniques in the first-year seminar associated with the service-learning component?*
- *Please describe how sections of the first-year seminar incorporate service learning.*

Respondents were asked to report how many hours students were required to complete as part of the service-learning component. A total of 31.3% of campuses indicated that students were required to complete five or fewer hours of service (Figure 19) That proportion increased to 50.3% of institutions when the required number of hours of service was increased to 10 or fewer. In addition, 42.4% reported there was no requirement about the total number of hours. Slightly more than one quarter (26.5%) of campuses required more than five hours of service, and only 6.3% required more than 10.

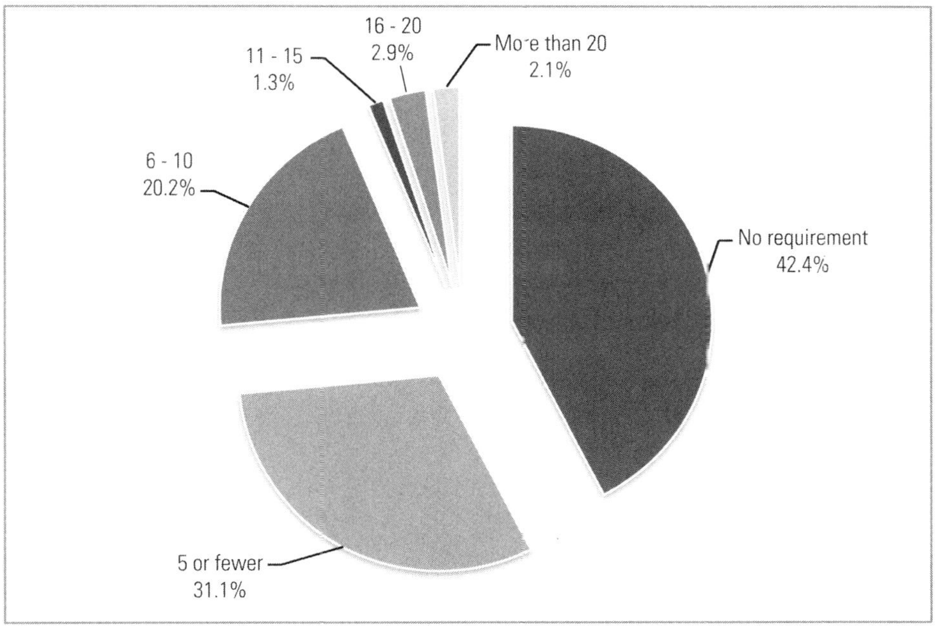

Figure 13. Total number of hours required for students engaged in service-learning in the first-year seminar (n = 238).

A few interesting differences emerged when service requirements were disaggregated by institutional characteristics. Public colleges and universities more frequently reported not having a specific hour requirement for service-learning, 49.5% compared to 36.8% at private institutions. When the responses were broken down by primary seminar type, those institutions with the majority of their first-year students in extended orientation or basic study skills seminars indicated most frequently that they require five hours or fewer in the service-learning component of the seminar, 42.7% and 42.9%, respectively. Campuses with the remaining primary seminar types most frequently reported they had no requirement for the number of hours students are expected to complete in their service experiences. The pattern of the distribution of responses for the number of required hours was similar for two- and four-year campuses.

Meaningful reflection is a critical component of service-learning (AAC&U, 2007; Eyler & Giles, 1999; Zlotkowski, 2002). Given that reflection is a sine qua non of the service-learning experience, institutions were asked to identify techniques used to reflect on the service-learning experiences in the first-year seminar. Open-ended responses to the 2009 NSFYS indicated that reflection following service opportunities was carried out through class discussions, papers, and presentations. Response options for the 2012-2013 administration were derived from these data. Class discussions (77.3%) and writing exercises (77.3%) were the predominant techniques used for reflecting on the service-learning component (Figure 20). Half of respondents reported that student presentations were used as a reflection, while slightly more than 20% reported portfolios were used. A small proportion (4.6%) of institutions that connect service-learning to the first-year seminar reported requiring no reflection.

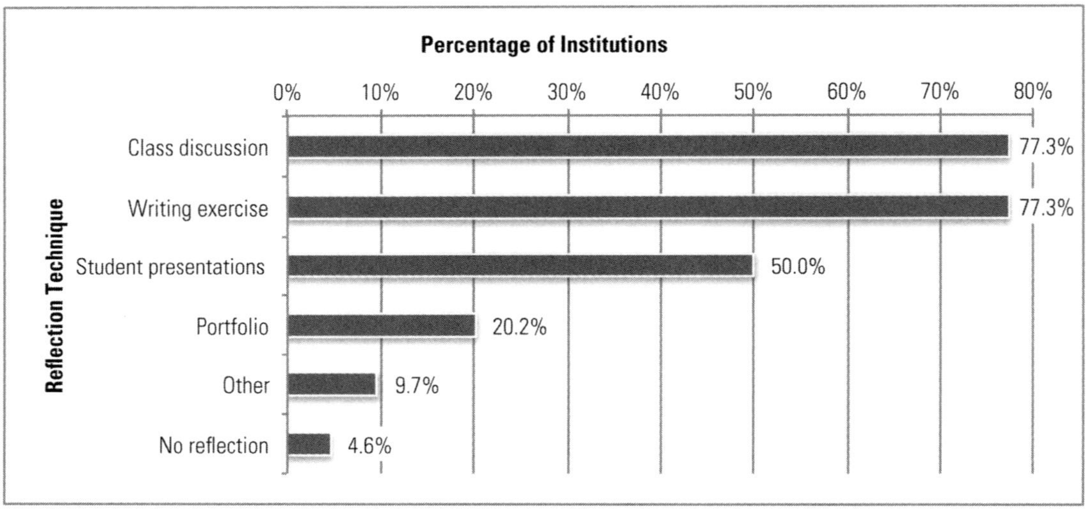

Figure 20. Reflection techniques associated with service-learning in the first-year seminar (*n* = 238). The sum of the percentages is larger than 100% due to the ability of respondents to select more than one response.

In general, the overall distribution of these responses was consistent when they were disaggregated by institutional characteristics, including type, control, size of incoming class, and primary seminar type. This held true for all institutional variables with the exception of the basic study skills seminar where the use of portfolios was the third most frequently reported reflection technique.

To offer more context and depth regarding service-learning in the first-year seminar, institutions were asked to provide an open-ended response describing how sections of the first-year seminar incorporated service-learning. Figure 21 presents the distribution of these responses.

One group of institutions reported that students were given freedom to choose the service-based project they would complete as an assignment in the seminar (13.6%). Another group of responses emphasized service-learning in connection with the institution. This group included institutions that identified service-learning connected to the seminar through institution-based days of service (5.1%), new student orientation (4.7%),

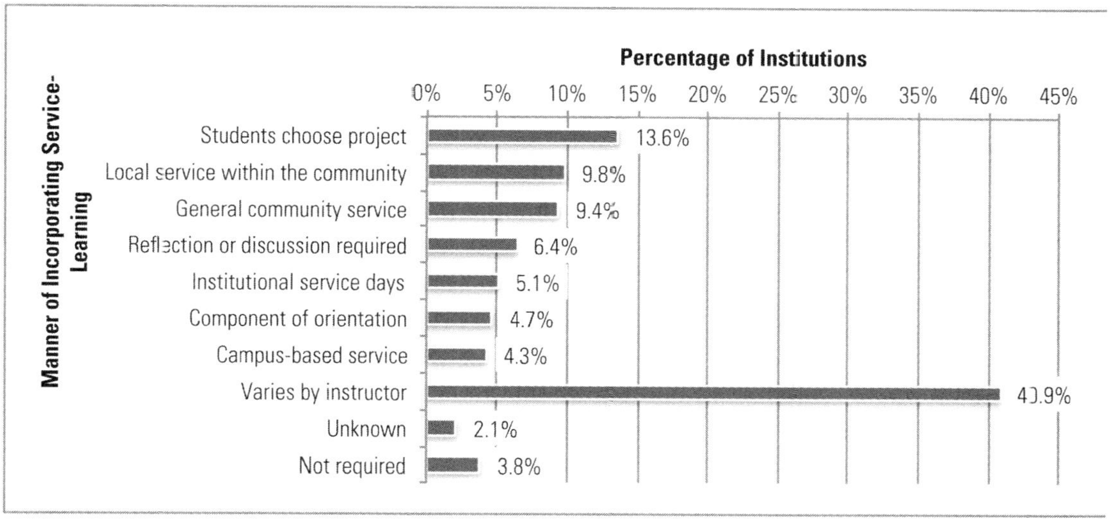

Figure 21. How the first-year seminar incorporates service-learning (n = 235).

or a service project that was organized by the institution (4.3%). Taken together, two categories, local service within the community (9.8%) and general community service (9.4%), represented students providing service to the community as a component of the service-learning experience in the seminar. Finally, 6.4% of responding institutions expressed that the service-learning component was incorporated in the seminar through a required reflection experience, such as a discussion.

The response that was far and away the most frequent was that the inclusion of service-learning varied by the course instructor—more than 40%. Undoubtedly, flexibility in the management and coordination of service-learning allows instructors to select experiences that best connect to the learning goals and needs of each section of the course. Yet, these responses, coupled with the absence of a requirement for the number of hours, suggest an inadequate structure for service-learning experiences.

Learning Communities

When AAC&U introduced HIPs, it defined learning communities as two or more linked courses in which students work closely with one another and faculty to explore ideas that have meaning beyond the classroom (AAC&U, 2007). The first-year seminar has increasingly appeared as one of the courses comprising learning communities (Henscheid, 2004); the proportion of respondents reporting sections linked to other courses has steadily increased since the 1994 administration of the NSFYS, growing from 17.2% in 1994 to 35.7% in 2009 (Barefoot & Fidler, 1996; Padgett & Keup, 2011; Tobolowsky & Associates, 2008).

In the 2009 administration, institutional representatives were asked to describe the learning community of which the first-year seminar was a part. Respondents described a variety of learning community structures, including freshman interest groups (FIGs) and living-learning communities, as well as support for various groups, such as honors, commuter, adult and new students (Padgett & Keup, 2011). These responses illustrated the complexity and diversity of the purposes, use, and structural features of the learning communities that included sections of the seminar.

To facilitate conversation and to identify similar types of learning communities, several typologies for their structures have been created (Inkelas & Longerbeam, 2008; Lenning & Ebbers, 1999; Love & Tokuno, 1999; MacGregor, Smith, Matthews, & Gabelnick, 1990; Shapiro & Levine, 1999; Snider & Venable, 2000; Stassen, 2003). A review of these typologies revealed several common features of learning communities: (a) a common cohort of students in two or more courses (Lenning & Ebbers, 1999; Love & Tokuno, 1999; MacGregor et al., 1990), (b) a common cohort of students in all courses (MacGregor et al., 1990; Snider & Venable, 2000), (c) coordination of content by instructors of the courses (Lenning & Ebbers, 1999; Love & Tokuno, 1999; MacGregor et al., 1990), (d) course content connected by a common theme (Love & Tokuno, 1999; MacGregor et al., 1990), (e) students gathering around academic topics outside the course (Love & Tokuno, 1999), and (f) residential or living-learning communities (Inkelas & Longerbeam, 2008; Lenning & Ebbers, 1999; Shapiro & Levine, 1999). These common features formed the basis of the question on this administration of the NSFYS about structural components of learning communities to which first-year seminars were connected. While these characteristics might expand beyond the definition of learning communities offered by AAC&U (2007), they were derived and included to yield responses that would be applicable and comparable to other research more broadly.

To that end, the most recent administration asked institutions to report features of the learning communities in which seminars were embedded. Further, the instrument included a free-response option allowing respondents to describe the role the learning community played in the seminar. This section will address the results gathered from these two questions.

Similar to the results reported from the 2009 administration (Padgett & Keup, 2011; Skipper & Keup, 2010), the most frequently identified feature of the learning community connected to the first-year seminar was student co-enrollment in the first-year seminar and one or more other courses, or linked courses (73.8%). This feature was reported at more than twice the rate of any other, making it far and away the most common type of learning community of which the seminar is part. Much less prevalent was a cohort structure, where seminar students took all of their classes together. Only 9.1% of campuses identified this as a feature of the learning community that included the seminar. The distribution of all features of learning communities connected to first-year seminars is presented in Figure 22.

In addition, roughly one third of respondents indicated that the course content in the first-year seminar and the linked course was intentionally coordinated (34.5%). Another prominent feature of these learning communities was the connection of the seminar to theme-based experiences outside the course (33.5%). Nearly a quarter (25.8%) of institutions indicated course content connected by a common theme as a characteristic of the learning community. Finally, the living-learning or residential learning community was reported by 30.5% of respondents as a feature that was connected to the first-year seminar on their campuses.

Some interesting results emerged when the features of learning communities were broken down by institutional characteristics. Co-enrollment in the first-year seminar and other courses increased along with the number of entering first-year students. Linked courses were identified as a feature of the learning community by 58.1% of institutions of less than 500 first-year students, and the proportion increased steadily by class size up to 86.4% of institutions with more than 4,000 students in the entering class. Likewise, the presence of living-learning communities on campuses increased with the size of the first-year class. The percentage of institutions reporting a living-learning community connected to the first-year seminar increased from 21.0% of campuses with less than 500 entering first-year students to 40.9% with more than 4,000.

More two-year (16.4% compared to 7.0% four-year) and public (11.1% compared to 5.8% private) institutions reported that the first-year seminar is part of a learning community in which students are co-enrolled in all courses. Not surprisingly, living-learning communities are much more prevalent at four-year campuses (38.3%) than at two-year campuses (3.3%).

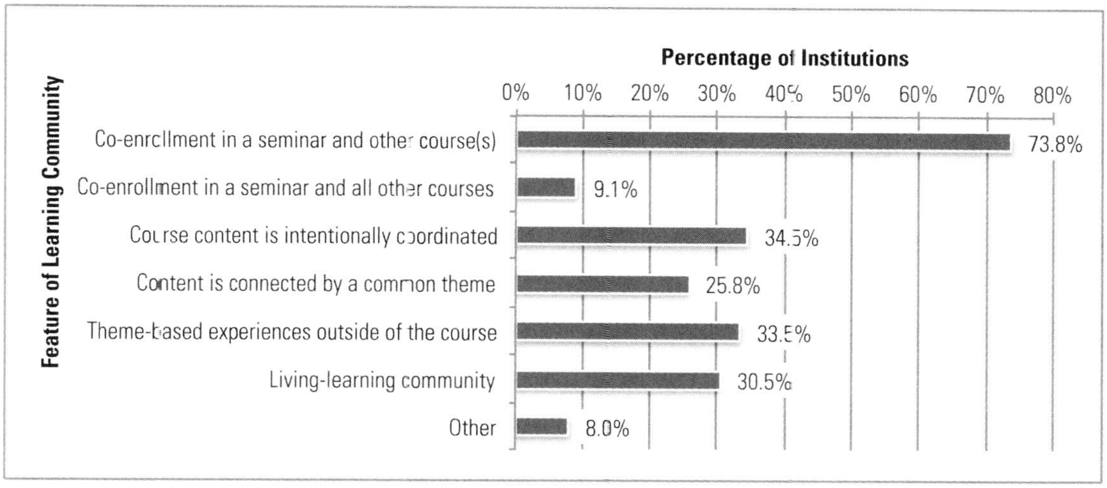

Figure 22. Features of learning communities connected to the first-year seminar (*n* = 275). The sum of the percentages is larger than 100% due to the ability of respondents to select more than one response.

As a follow-up to the question about the features of learning communities, participants were asked to describe the role of the first-year seminar. Responses to this open-ended question were grouped together based on common themes and are displayed in Figure 23. The most frequently identified role of the learning community in the first-year seminar reiterated that the seminar was linked with other common courses. The learning community also played an important role in developing students' sense of belonging by connecting them to their peers (17.6%), to an academic discipline or theme (16.2%), and to the campus and its resources (12.5%). A group of responding institutions (10.3%) indicated that the first-year seminar itself was the central feature of the learning community. Finally, 14 (5.1%) institutions noted the seminar and the learning community worked together to support students enrolled in developmental courses on the campus.

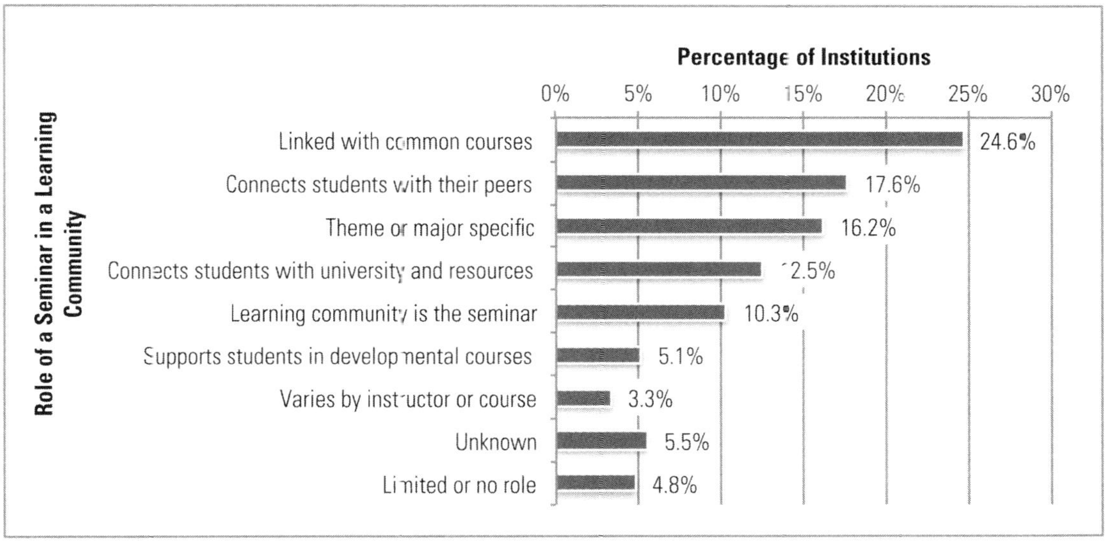

Figure 23. The role of the first-year seminar in the learning community (*n* = 272).

Common Reading Experiences

The survey included one open-ended follow-up question asking how the first-year seminar incorporates the common reading experience. As exhibited in Figure 24, most institutions reported that the reading formed the basis of in-class experiences, including discussions (32.6%) or papers and presentations (10.9%). The common reading experience was also reported as a mechanism to connect students to other campus activities, such as orientation or convocation (15.4%), or as the basis for connecting the first-year seminar to other courses in a learning community (1.1%), which is consistent with the description of common intellectual experiences by AAC&U (Kuh, 2008). Responding institutions also reported the common reading was used to inform the curriculum of the first-year seminar either by its use as the required text for the course (15.8%) or by serving as a theme for the seminar (4.9%).

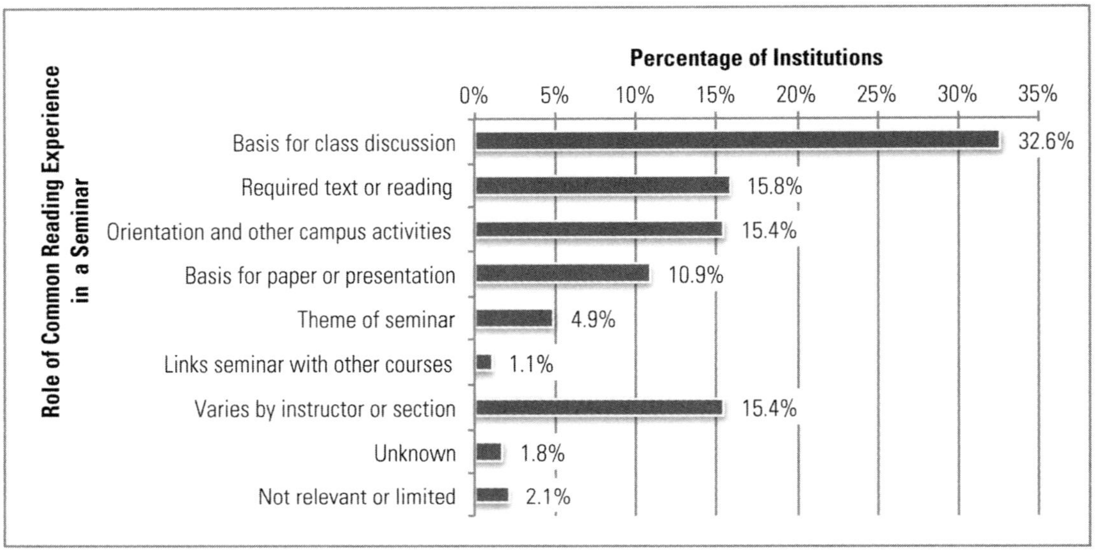

Figure 24. How the first-year seminar incorporates the common reading experience ($n = 285$).

Undergraduate Research

Finally, institutions had the opportunity to describe the integration of undergraduate research in the seminar by responding to an open-ended question on the subject. Figure 25 presents the responses, which were analyzed and grouped according to common themes. When undergraduate research is connected to the first-year seminar, its most frequently reported use is to develop research skills (17.7%) or information literacy (11.5%). Many institutions also described the seminar as an outlet for undergraduate research products, such as papers as assignments (14.6%) or presentations on research (13.5%). Seminars were also named as places where students would identify an avenue of self-directed research (10.4%). Approximately 11% of campuses mentioned sections for students in specific disciplines (8.3%) or the honors program (3.1%) as the place where undergraduate research and the first-year seminar connected. A large number of respondents (17.7%) reported the inclusion of undergraduate research in the first-year seminar was at the discretion of instructors or specific disciplines.

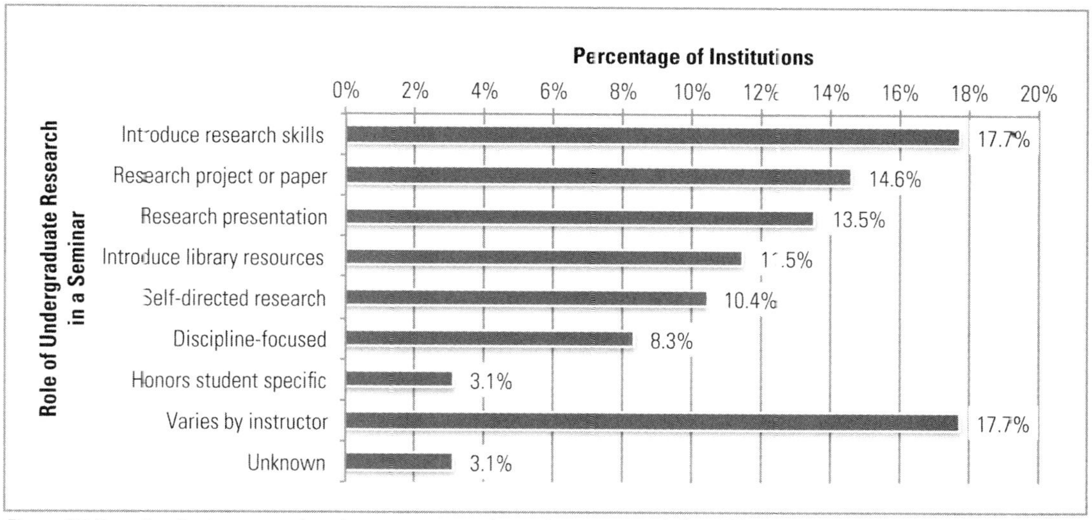

Figure 25. How the first-year seminar incorporates undergraduate research (*n* = 96).

Conclusion

It is prudent to step back at this point and reflect on what these results suggest. More than 9 out of 10 institutions reported offering one of the high-impact activities named by AAC&U in connection with the first-year seminar. The median response of the number of educationally effective practices in the seminar is three. As the first-year seminar is a high-impact practice itself, students who enroll in these courses are likely exposed to a total of two educationally effective practices at nearly all institutions and potentially as many as four. This is above the recommendation by Kuh (2008) that undergraduates should participate in one high-impact practice in the lower division, or the equivalent of the first two years of enrollment. While this result does not speak to how widespread these opportunities are or the quality of the educationally focused practices, it implies that the first-year seminar serves as a central connection point for delivering them to students.

Discussion and Implications

The 2012-2013 National Survey of First-Year Seminars (NSFYS), as with previous administrations, provided a snapshot of the practices related to curricular interventions aimed at supporting first-year student success. As a thorough discussion of each result presented in the previous section is not practical, here we discuss selected findings and the implications of the same. In particular, this discussion focuses on academic rigor in the seminar, the use of contingent instructors, the role of undergraduate peer educators, and the incorporation of high-impact educational practices in the first-year seminar.

Increasing Academic Rigor

Since the first administration of the NSFYS in 1988, the percentage of responding institutions reporting the presence of a first-year seminar has increased from 68.5% (Tobolowsky & Associates, 2008) to 89.7% in the current administration. The proportion of campuses reporting academic seminars as the primary seminar type (i.e., the seminar with the highest student enrollment) has also increased. Conversely, the number of institutions reporting the extended orientation as the primary seminar type has been decreasing. The 2012-2013 NSFYS marks the first time the extended orientation and academic seminars, both uniform and variable content across sections, were listed as primary seminars at nearly the same rate. While it cannot be demonstrated that academic seminars have accounted for the increase in the overall adoption of first-year seminars, academic seminars have outpaced the growth of any other type over the past 25 years.

In addition, the results of the 2012-2013 National Survey show that academic seminars are more likely to have their credits applied toward general education requirements, have more classroom contact hours, and have more HIPs connected to them. It is possible and likely that institutions see academically focused seminars as more legitimate than other types, which could explain their growth in prevalence and their inclusion in the core curriculum. However, the connection of more HIPs to academic seminars than other types leads to another explanation: the growing prevalence of academic first-year seminars signals an increase of rigor in the first-year curriculum. In other words, it is possible that more academic seminars are offered in response to charges of a lack of rigor in higher education, particularly in the first college year.

Several groups have pointed to the importance of having high standards for students in the undergraduate curriculum. For example, Chickering and Gamson (1987) outlined a set of principles of good practice in undergraduate education that included high expectations for students. Soon after, the Wingspread Group (1993) called for increased academic rigor in what it referred to as a "trivialized" undergraduate education. Upcraft, Gardner, and Barefoot (2005) echoed this, highlighting the evidence that college was less demanding than students expected and suggesting that institutions respond by intentionally increasing the level of challenge for first-year students. Results from Project DEEP (Kuh et al., 2005) showed that institutions with higher-than-predicted levels of student engagement maintained developmentally appropriate standards of excellence. That is, students who were asked to stretch to meet higher performance expectations worked to rise to the occasion.

It is important for first-year seminars of any type to provide students with an appropriate level of challenge. First-year seminars have been developed with the objectives of connecting students to the institution, providing an orientation to campus resources and services, and developing academic skills (see earlier discussion on course objectives and topics). Implicit in these goals is a larger objective that the seminar will set students up for success for the rest of their time in college. In her keynote address at the 2013 Annual Conference on the First-Year Experience, Jillian Kinzie issued a challenge that students be held to a high standard and that educators should not back away from this expectation. She cited findings from the National Survey of Student Engagement (NSSE) suggesting research that students will rise to meet the challenge. Students will not be well prepared for the challenges they will face in the remainder of their academic career and beyond if there are low expectations in courses they take when they first arrive on campus, including the first-year seminar.

This call to action is especially important in institutional contexts where nonacademic seminar types, such as extended orientation or basic study skills, have been determined the most appropriate for first-year students. With increasing criticism about the cost of college attendance and time to degree, programs have been required to demonstrate their contributions to student outcomes or face the possibility of being discontinued. Academic seminars might be less susceptible to this criticism, as they are, by nature, more like other courses in a student's schedule and their credits are applied more frequently toward general education requirements. Nonetheless, it is important to the long-term survival of the first-year seminar on any campus to be able to demonstrate its contribution to the academic success of the students enrolled.

Contingent Instructors

Contingent or contract faculty are instructors who are in part-time appointments or are not on the tenure track, such as graduate assistants, postdoctoral researchers, and staff employed by colleges and universities in nonacademic roles (Eagan & Jaeger, 2008). These instructors have been growing in number since the mid-20th century (Schuster & Finkelstein, 2006) and now represent nearly half of all faculty employed by institutions of higher education (Schuster & Finkelstein, 2007).

While tenure-track faculty was the professional role most frequently reported (71.1%) by campuses as the instructor for the seminar, more than half of institutions reported the use of contingent faculty to instruct the course, including full-time, non-tenure-track (60.7%) and adjunct (51.9%) faculty as well as student affairs and other campus professionals (54.7%). Distinct patterns of professional role of instructors emerged when the responses were disaggregated by institutional characteristics. Two-year and public institutions were significantly more likely to identify adjunct faculty as the instructors of the seminar ($p < .001$). Furthermore, the distribution of responses regarding instructor professional role differed based on the institution's primary seminar type as both types of academic (uniform and variable content across sections) and preprofessional or discipline-linked seminars identified tenure-track faculty most often. Campuses with basic study skills as the primary type of seminar most frequently reported the use of adjunct faculty, and those with extended orientation identified student affairs professionals as the predominant professional role of instructors.

Based on these results, it is clear that first-year seminars are heavily reliant on tenure-track faculty as well as contingent instructors, namely adjunct and tenure ineligible faculty and campus professionals. Contingent faculty allow institutions a cost-effective and efficient approach to employing instructors (Eagan & Jaeger, 2008; Schuster & Finkelstein, 2006). This is particularly important at institutions that require a large number of their first-year students to enroll in a seminar. Schuster and Finkelstein (2006) suggested that contingent faculty also provide potential benefits to campuses in that they may be more responsive than tenure-track faculty to the needs of diverse student populations, especially students who work full-time and attend college part-time.

At the same time, recent research has demonstrated deleterious effects on outcomes among students who are in classrooms led by contingent faculty. Jaeger (2008) found that students' exposure to contingent faculty had negative effects on such outcomes as persistence and graduation rates. Further evidence has demonstrated that community college students' exposure to contingent faculty had negative effects on the rates at which they transferred to a four-year institution (Eagan & Jaeger, 2009; Jaeger, 2008). Moreover, there was evidence that the negative effects were more pronounced with increased exposure (Eagan & Jaeger, 2009). This presents a particularly worrisome problem as approximately 48% of community college students' credit hours are spent in courses with contingent faculty (Jaeger, 2008). Umbach (2007) noted similar results and found that contingent faculty interacted less frequently with students, used active and collaborative techniques less often, spent less time preparing for class, and had lower academic expectations than tenure-track faculty.

Both Umbach (2007) and Jaeger (2008) conceded that contingent faculty are beneficial to the institution and that they likely underperform because of the lack of support received from the institution in areas such as office space and information technology. Additionally, many part-time faculty members are employed at multiple institutions and have limited time to meet with students outside class (Eagan & Jaeger, 2008). Campus staff, such as student affairs professionals, may not face some of the same challenges, such as space and technology, as part-time faculty employed outside of the institution where the course is taught. Nevertheless, more institutions reported that faculty (of all types) taught the seminar as part of their assigned work (74.9%) than staff (40.1%).[2] Accordingly, fewer respondents indicated that faculty taught as an additional responsibility (47.6%) than staff (72.2%). Thus, staff who instruct the seminar must more frequently find time outside their work commitments to develop lesson plans, meet with the students, and teach the course.

Compounding this problem, campuses with basic study skills as the primary type of seminar most frequently reported the use of adjunct faculty. Institutions reporting basic study skills as the primary type most frequently require students who are academically underprepared or enrolled in developmental or remedial courses to take the seminar. Students who enroll in remedial coursework are a vulnerable population on campus, experiencing delays to graduation and having a lower probability of graduating (Attewell, Lavin, Domina, & Levey, 2006). Additional studies that examine the interaction of the dual exposure to contingent faculty and developmental and remedial coursework on student outcomes can shed light on how institutions can adequately support students and instructors involved in basic study skills seminars.

We concede that the contingent faculty in these studies includes those who teach in all types of courses and are not focused on the first-year seminar specifically. Future research should examine the effects of the use of contingent instructors in first-year seminars on student outcomes. Since there are several types of seminars and a different distribution of instructor types within each the interaction of the effects of instructor professional role and seminar type on student outcomes needs to be studied in further detail.

It is important to note that by bringing these results to light we do not suggest that contingent instructors, such as adjunct faculty, staff, or graduate students, are not important contributors to the first-year seminar; it is quite the opposite. The results of the survey demonstrate that institutions rely on instructors from a wide range of professional roles to meet the needs of the students enrolled in first-year seminars. These so called "contingent" instructors play a vital part in the success of whatever type of seminar they teach. However, it is incumbent upon the institution to provide appropriate support for these instructors so that the benefits coming from student participation in the seminars are not negated.

For the seminar to be most effective, instructors must be given the tools they need to succeed. Those instructors who are teaching the seminar as a responsibility in addition to their primary professional role might require additional support, including meeting space, access to technology, training, lesson planning resources, and dedicated time to prepare for class and to meet with students.

Peer Educators

The good news is that the 2012-2013 NSFYS has provided a better estimate of the prevalence of the use of student peer educators in the first-year seminar than previous administrations of the survey. As mentioned earlier in this report, the high-water mark for the estimated percentage of undergraduate students serving in an educational role in the first-year seminar was 10.0% in the 2000 administration of the survey. This figure dropped to an all-time low of 5.1% in 2009. Based on a change in the branching pattern in the 2012-2013 administration, 46.3% of campuses reported undergraduates served in some way as a peer educator in the first-year seminar.

[2] These results can be found in Appendix D of this report. See distribution of responses to Q29 and Q30.

The power of peers as educators cannot be overstated. Astin (1993) succinctly summed this up when he stated "the student's peer group is the single most potent source of influence on growth and development" (p. 398). Peer educators in the first-year seminar have the potential to be powerful agents for the development of first-year students in the classroom and beyond. Positive academic peer interactions lead to gains in knowledge acquisition and academic skill development (Astin, 1993; Landrum & Nelson, 2002; Lewis & Lewis, 2005; Pascarella & Terenzini, 2005). Furthermore, peer mentorship contributes to students' sense of belonging at an institution (Hill & Reddy, 2007; Jacobi, 1991; Nora & Crisp, 2007). Additionally, students who work with peer educators are more likely to be referred to appropriate campus services in a timely manner (Cuseo, 1991; Grosz, 1990; Kram & Isabella, 1985; Sharkin, Plageman, & Mangold, 2003). The most influential peer interactions on student learning are those that reinforce the academic program and extend it into nonclassroom settings (Pascarella & Terenzini, 2005).

While it was good news to find that undergraduates were being used more frequently in first-year seminars than previously thought, the majority of campuses reported that undergraduates did not play a role in the first-year seminar. This was even more pronounced on two-year campuses, where 9 out of 10 two-year colleges report not using peer educators in the first-year seminar. At a structural level, the use of peers in the seminar is challenging in two-year institutions, which do not have upper-division students. Also, two-year colleges enroll more part-time students (Provasnik & Planty, 2008), who are less likely to spend time on campus and more likely to have commitments outside of school. If students are enrolled full-time, their tenure on campus is short, with most staying only a few terms beyond the entering cohort. In addition, students on two-year campuses tend to be more transient, with large numbers of students transferring in and out (Borden, 2004). Further research should examine the opportunities and obstacles for the use of undergraduate peer leaders in first-year seminars.

The use of undergraduate peer leaders is an area of opportunity for all institutions, and particularly rich for two-year and public colleges and universities. Returning students who have found unique ways to navigate the institution, particularly those part-time students with other obligations, such as work and family, would be a helpful resource for first-year students from all backgrounds. Involving transfer students, who tend to be less engaged than students who started their academic careers at the same institution (Kinzie, 2013), as peer educators in the seminar not only serves to benefit entering students but also gives them an avenue to find a connection to the campus.

High-Impact Practices in the First-Year Seminar

Since the introduction and identification of high-impact practices (HIPs) by AAC&U in 2007, there has been discussion and evidence that the first-year seminar serves as a curricular anchor for these activities on campuses (Greenfield et al., 2013; Kuh et al., 2005). Findings from the 2012-2013 NSFYS confirm this belief. More than 90% of institutions reported offering at least one HIP, and 76% reported offering at least two connected to the first-year seminar. Furthermore, more than half of all colleges and universities reported offering three of these educationally purposeful activities in connection to the seminar. In other words, the average student enrolled in a first-year seminar will be exposed to an opportunity to participate in four HIPS during his or her first year of college. This is greater than the recommendation by Kuh (2008) that undergraduates should participate in one of these activities in the first two years.

The first-year seminar has been historically connected to service-learning, common reading, and learning communities. However, only 30% to 40% of participating institutions reported connecting these HIPS to the seminar. A review of the responses related to the structure of these initiatives raises questions about the quality of the connection.

Estimates by Barefoot et al. (2012) indicated that nearly 40% of first-year students in four-year colleges participate in service-learning. Further, their results showed that the first-year participation rate is higher than students with any other class standing. Nearly one third of respondents to the 2012-2013 NSFYS (31.8%) reported connecting service-learning to the first-year seminar. One promising result related to service-learning was that more than three quarters of institutions reported using class discussions or writing exercises as reflection techniques in the service component of the seminar. Requiring students to engage in meaningful reflection connected to the experience is a widely accepted standard for differentiating service-learning from community service (AAC&U, 2007; Eyler & Giles, 1999; Zlotkowski, 2002). However, the additional information provided by respondents did not demonstrate the intentionality of the service component in the seminar. More than two out of every five institutions reported that no specific duration of service was required of students. Where a minimum number of hours was identified, more than half of campuses reported mandating 10 hours or fewer, a requirement that could be easily accomplished in one or two days. Similarly, more than 40% of responses to the open-ended question indicated that the inclusion of service-learning in the seminar was left to the individual instructor's discretion. Such approaches reveal a pattern where structures aimed at creating an educationally purposeful activity are not present or are weak at best. More investigation is warranted to determine whether colleges and universities are simply providing opportunities for service or volunteerism in the first-year seminar and calling it service-learning or if service is an educationally purposeful activity integrated into the curriculum of the course in which application and reflection (AAC&U, 2007) are happening in intentional ways.

Information about the connection of the first-year seminar to learning communities has been gathered since the 1994 administration of the NSFYS. The concept of a learning community in these administrations was simply the linking of the first-year seminar to another course in the students' schedules. The prevalence of this linked-course learning community rose from 17.5% of institutions in 1994 (Tobolowsky & Associates, 2008) to 35.7% in 2009 (Padgett & Keup, 2011). The 2012-2013 administration included a set of features of learning communities to which first-year seminars were connected. The predominant feature reported by a large majority of institutions was that students were co-enrolled in the first-year seminar and one or more other linked courses. Only one third of institutions reported the seminar and the linked courses had intentionally coordinated content; a quarter of campuses, that were not mutually exclusive, indicated they were connected by a common theme.

Henscheid (2004) described two roles that the first-year seminar might play within a learning community: (a) synthesizing learning across courses or (b) serving as a site for building community. Most institutions described the learning community as simply the common enrollment of students in the first-year seminar and another course on campus, which falls in line with the community-building function of the learning community. A smaller number of respondents described the learning community as a place for the synthesis of learning by outlining common content, themes, or goals across the linked courses. More research is warranted to better understand these linked courses and how they are structured to support cognitive and social development of the students enrolled in them.

Laufgraben (2006) suggested that effective common reading initiatives are structured to model academic behavior, set expectations for student success, foster involvement, and promote more meaningful learning. The responses to the open-ended questions about this practice provided evidence that common reading experiences connected to the first-year seminar were intentionally designed to provide at least some of these experiences for students. A fair number of institutions described a thoughtful and purposeful approach to integrating this common intellectual experience by including the themes from the reading in discussions, assignments, and experiences during the first-year seminar. Others described a pre-enrollment reading experience with a discussion during orientation that was connected to the first-year seminar. However, many described a loose connection between the common reading experience and the seminar. For example, many respondents described a single discussion of the text during the term of the course. This kind of approach does not use the initiative to its fullest potential; without intentional and systematic integration of the common intellectual experience repeated throughout the first-year curriculum, or at least the seminar, the opportunities for students to engage each other around the experience are left to chance.

The most frequently reported educationally effective practices were collaborative assignments (67.2%) and diversity (58.8%), notwithstanding differences in the proportion of institutions offering these two HIPs based on certain institutional characteristics. It is interesting that the predominant practices connected to the first-year seminar focus on improving students' ability to understand and to work with those with different backgrounds and life experiences (AAC&U, 2007). However, while these two practices were the most frequently reported HIPs offered in connection with the first-year seminar, the objectives and topics focused on developing intercultural competence, diversity, global learning, and student support networks were among those least frequently identified as most important by respondents. This raises the question of whether administrators at colleges and universities are creating purposeful connections between educationally effective practices or are simply checking off items on a list of desired activities. Additional research is needed on the degree or quality of the integration of pedagogical approaches related to diversity and collaborative learning in the first-year seminar.

What this review of responses suggests when taken together is that many institutions are simply layering practices on top of each other rather than intentionally weaving them together to form a focused, intentional educational environment. While these connected activities might provide some mutual benefit to students, one wonders whether these institutions are doing them well (Kuh, 2008) or simply doing them. These findings point to the need for further research to investigate the depth and quality of the integration of these educationally effective approaches in the first-year seminar. This will shed light on the question of whether these practices in combination create the "single multidimensional activity" that Kuh (2010, p. xiii) describes.

Of particular interest was the finding that two-year colleges were less likely to offer HIPs in connection with first-year seminars. These institutions offered significantly fewer of these practices overall and significantly fewer of the five included in the survey. This brings up concerns about the equity of educationally purposeful approaches for the students who attend these institutions. HIPs have been demonstrated to lead to important student outcomes, such as academic success, persistence to the second year, engagement, and deep learning, particularly for those students from historically underserved backgrounds (AAC&U, 2007; Kuh, 2008). Such students are more likely to enroll in two-year institutions. Thus, the students who stand to gain the most from these types of educational activities are less likely to have the opportunity to engage in them in conjunction with the first-year seminar.

In his description of HIPs and their benefit to students, Kuh (2008) issued the challenge that colleges and universities must make participating in educationally purposeful activities a reality and a priority for every student. It is important to note that the presence of these activities in the first-year seminars does not necessarily denote student participation. Many responses indicated that the implementation and structure of HIPs were left to instructor discretion. It is also likely that students have the choice to opt into (or not) these experiences. Thus, while service-learning may be a component of a seminar on campus, it may very well be optional. Even if the HIP is a nonoptional part of the first-year seminar, wide variance may exist in its structure and implementation across individual sections, making it difficult for campuses to assess its impact on student learning and other relevant outcomes.

Further research is needed to investigate the prevalence of these practices in each specific section of the seminars on campus to be able to speak to the overall exposure of students to these activities. This research should also take into account key student characteristics, especially those students who stand to benefit the most from participation in these effective educational activities. Such studies would be able to shed light on many questions that remain unanswered. Are students from certain backgrounds self-selecting into seminars with HIPs connected to them at different rates? Are students who are most vulnerable, such as students in developmental education programs, being required to engage in learning communities connecting the first-year seminar to other remedial courses, or are they opting to avoid them? Do first-generation students have the cultural capital to know that they stand to benefit from the very practices that have been shown to have greater impact for historically underserved populations, such as participation in first-year seminars or other HIPs?

The first-year seminar is a natural and efficient central situating point for HIPs and other educationally effective practices, such as student involvement and peer leadership. When considering initiatives that would combine these activities, we echo Kuh's statement, "to engage students at high levels, these practices must be done well" (2008, p. 20). If given the choice between quantity and quality, the latter should prevail. However, at an institutional level, it is possible to have both. The quantity is important because it provides a variety of opportunities to meet each student's needs and interests. The quality is important because it delivers on the promise of the impact these practices have been proven to provide.

25 Years Later: The Case for Continuing the NSFYS

While the survey has been administered nine times over 25 years, and the 2012-2013 NSFYS provided more evidence about the prevalence of the first-year seminar nationally as well as its structure and practice, there is still much to learn about these curricular-based initiatives. For example, are institutions consciously changing the type of seminar they are offering? So far, we have been able to identify trends but are only able to speculate about the reasons for the changes. Similarly, the NSFYS has not yet gathered information about the institutional policy environment and how it affects the structure and characteristics of seminars on campus.

The NSFYS is limited by the design of the questionnaire, which asks institutions to report on the seminar type with highest student enrollment. It is possible to imagine a scenario in which a campus has two strong seminars with roughly equal enrollments or highly effective seminars designed to serve small, but unique, segments of the campus community. As such, the survey does not fully capture the complexity of the efforts designed to serve incoming first-year students.

Finally, the National Survey of First-Year Seminars has focused solely on one innovation in the first college year. Are there other first-year experience programs serving students in educationally powerful ways that are not, like the first-year seminar, course-based? Are we missing out on learning valuable lessons about approaches that serve students well because of the history of the first-year seminar in the first-year experience movement? Are we also creating or perpetuating a norm that the seminar is the preferred first-year initiative by focusing the national survey only on the seminar?

Conclusion

The 2012-2013 NSFYS provided an updated national overview of the characteristics of the first-year seminar. Informative patterns emerged when the data were disaggregated by institutional characteristics. As such, institutions can use the results as a comparative tool against the current snapshot of the first-year seminar nationwide. While these national data should serve as a guide to inform decision makers, each institution provides a unique context. The first-year seminar serves a purpose specific to the setting, which includes a unique combination of students, mission, and goals. While it might be possible to use the results from the survey to craft a seminar with all the most commonly reported features, this seminar is certain to fail on at least some level. These results are most successfully used to inspire institutions to create, revise, or adapt a course-based intervention that will contribute to the ongoing achievement of their first-year students.

Appendix A: Survey Methodology

Population

The population for the 2012-2013 National Survey of the First-Year Seminars (NSFYS) were chief academic officers (CAOs), chief executive officers (CEOs), and/or chief student affairs officers (CSAOs) at regionally accredited, undergraduate-serving institutions of higher education, listed in the *Higher Education Directory*. The CAOs, CEOs, and/or CSAOs were contacted via e-mail and asked to forward the invitation to participate if it was more appropriate for another person on their campus to complete the survey. Giving contacts the instruction to forward the questionnaire was designed to ensure that the respondents would be those individuals who were the most knowledgeable about the first-year seminar at each institution.

Survey Administration

The questionnaire was created and constructed by the National Resource Center for The First-Year Experience and Students in Transition (NRC). The dissemination and administration of this survey was conducted using web-based survey technology developed and housed by CampusLabs.

Administration of the survey began on November 5, 2012. The first wave of invitations was sent to CAOs, or the CEOs if there was no listing for the CAO within the *Higher Education Directory*. If neither the CAO nor CEO was listed in the *Higher Education Directory*, the institution was omitted from the study. Nonverified or undeliverable e-mail accounts were also omitted from the study. The invitation served three main purposes: to (a) notify participates that the NRC was conducting an administration of the survey; (b) provide detailed information about when they could anticipate receiving a link to the survey instrument; and (c) confirm that the participant was the appropriate contact and representative who could accurately provide information about the first-year seminar, and if not, request the correct campus contact information.

At survey launch, 3,753 institutions were invited to participate. The institutions were e-mailed the survey link and given until December 17, 2012, to participate. Following the launch date, four follow-up reminders were sent to nonrespondents. The first reminder e-mail was sent to the CAO; the second reminder e-mail was sent to the CEO; and the third reminder e-mail was sent to all three institutional contacts (i.e., CAOs, CEOs, and CSAOs). The fourth and final e-mail was sent to all the institutional contacts who had responded to the 2009 survey but had not yet participated in the 2012-2013 survey administration. The deadline was extended to January 31, 2013, to allow the latter group sufficient time to participate. The survey link was officially disabled at noon EST on January 31, 2013.

Analyses

The analyses of the sample data were primarily conducted at the descriptive level. Comprehensive frequency distribution and sample percentages for each item reported throughout the research brief were tabulated for the sample in the aggregate (total) across institutional type, control, size, and seminar type. Note that significant effects are reported throughout the research brief. The majority of items included in the research report were categorical variables. Analyses for significance for these items were conducted using the chi-square test for fit of distribution. A fundamental assumption of the chi-square test is that there are adequate expected cell counts, which is at least 20% of the cells with expected counts of five or more. As a conservative approach to this assumption, analyses were not conducted when any actual cell counts were less than five. We have noted where such analyses were not conducted in tables throughout the report. With some ordinal-level items, for instance size of the incoming first-year class, the chi-square test was deemed appropriate because the interest was on the overall distribution of responses rather than determining differences in overall magnitude of the size of the first-year class when disaggregated by variables such as institution type or control or when used to disaggregate other items. Classroom contact hours was the only item with ordinal data that were not analyzed using the chi-square test. Because the interest was in the differences in the number of classroom contact hours by various institutional variables, such as type, control, and primary first-year seminar type, a Kruskal-Wallis H analysis was used.

Appendix B: Survey Instrument

2012-2013 National Survey on First-Year Seminars

This survey is intended to gather information regarding first-year seminars. The survey should take 30-45 minutes to complete. You may exit the survey at any time and return, and your responses will be saved.

In particular, you will be asked questions about the following related to first-year seminar on your campus:

- General institutional characteristics
- Types of first-year seminars offered
- Specific seminar information
- Student characteristics
- Instructor characteristics
- Administration of the seminar
- The course
- High-impact educational practices
- Assessment and evaluation practices

If you would like a copy of your responses, you will need to print each page of your survey before moving on to the next page.

Your responses are important to us, so please complete by December 17, 2012. Thank you.

1. Full name of institution: ____________________

2. City: ____________________

3. State: ____________________

4. Your first name: ____________________

5. Your last name: ____________________

6. Title: ____________________

7. E-mail address: ____________________

8. Please indicate the category that best describes your institution's type:
   - ❐ Two-year institution
   - ❐ Four-year institution

9. Please indicate the category that best describes your institution's control:
   - ❐ Public
   - ❐ Private, not-for-profit
   - ❐ Private, for-profit

10. Please indicate which of the following special designations apply to your institution: (Select all that apply.)
   - ❐ Tribal College or University
   - ❐ American Indian-Serving Institution (Non-Tribal College or University)
   - ❐ Asian American and Native American Pacific Islander-Serving Institution
   - ❐ Historically Black College or University (HBCU)
   - ❐ Black-Serving Institution (Non-HBCU)
   - ❐ Hispanic-Serving Institution
   - ❐ Other minority-serving institution
   - ❐ Military institution
   - ❐ Single-sex institution
   - ❐ Other special designation (please specify): ______________________________

11. What is the approximate number of entering first-year students in academic year 2012-2013 at your institution?
   - ❐ Less than 500 students
   - ❐ 501-1,000 students
   - ❐ 1,001-1,500 students
   - ❐ 1,501-2,000 students
   - ❐ 2,001-2,500 students
   - ❐ 2,501-3,000 students
   - ❐ 3,001-3,500 students
   - ❐ 3,501-4,000 students
   - ❐ 4,001-5,000 students
   - ❐ More than 5,000 students

First-year seminars are courses designed to enhance the academic skills and/or social development of first-year college students.

12. Does your institution, including any department or division, currently offer one or more first-year seminars?
   - ❐ Yes [*Go to Question 17*]
   - ❐ No
   - ❐ I don't know

13. Has your institution ever offered one or more first-year seminars?

- ❐ Yes
- ❐ No
- ❐ I don't know

14. Indicate the reason(s) why your institution does not currently offer a first-year seminar: (Select all that apply.)

- ❐ First-year issues are not an institutional priority
- ❐ Lack of expertise
- ❐ Lack of funding
- ❐ Lack of staff or faculty buy-in
- ❐ Limited time
- ❐ Other (please specify) ______________________________

15. Is your institution considering or developing a first-year seminar?

- ❐ Yes
- ❐ No
- ❐ I don't know

16. Which of the following high-impact educational practices does your institution offer for first-year students? (Select all that apply.)

- ❐ **Common Reading Experience** – First-year reading experience or summer reading program
- ❐ **Learning Community** – Linking a cohort of students in two or more courses or to a common set of theme-based experiences
- ❐ **Service-Learning** – Nonremunerative service as part of a course
- ❐ **Undergraduate Research** – Scientific inquiry, creative activity, or scholarship guided by a mentor from the faculty or research staff

[Go to Q80]

17. What is the approximate percentage of first-year students who take a first-year seminar on your campus?

- ❐ Less than 10%
- ❐ 10-19%
- ❐ 20-29%
- ❐ 30-39%
- ❐ 40-49%
- ❐ 50-59%
- ❐ 60-69%
- ❐ 70-79%
- ❐ 80-89%
- ❐ 90-99%
- ❐ 100%

18. Approximately how many years has a first-year seminar been offered on your campus?

- ❒ 2 years or less
- ❒ 3-5 years
- ❒ 6-10 years
- ❒ 11-15 years
- ❒ 16-20 years
- ❒ More than 20 years

Types of Seminars Offered

19. Select each discrete type of first-year seminar that best describes the seminars existing on your campus: (Select all that apply.)

- ❒ **Extended orientation seminar**—Sometimes called freshman orientation, college survival, college transition, or student success course. Content often includes introduction to campus resources, time management, academic and career planning, learning strategies, and an introduction to student development issues.
- ❒ **Academic seminar with generally uniform academic content across sections**—May be an interdisciplinary or theme-oriented course, sometimes part of a general education requirement. Primary focus is on academic theme or discipline, but will often include academic skills components, such as critical thinking and expository writing.
- ❒ **Academic seminar on various topics**—Similar to previously mentioned academic seminar except that specific topics vary from section to section.
- ❒ **Preprofessional or discipline-linked seminar**—Designed to prepare students for the demands of the major or discipline and the profession. Generally taught within professional schools or specific disciplines, such as engineering, health sciences, business, or education.
- ❒ **Basic study skills seminar**—Offered for academically underprepared students. The focus is on basic academic skills, such as grammar, note taking, and reading texts.
- ❒ **Hybrid**—Has elements from two or more type of seminars.
- ❒ Other

20. Please describe the hybrid first-year seminar: *[If "Hybrid" is selected for Question 19]*

21. Please describe the other first-year seminar: *[If "Other" is selected for Question 19]*

Specific Seminar Information

22. Which of the following first-year seminars has the highest student enrollment at your institution?

- ❐ Extended orientation seminar
- ❐ Academic seminar with generally uniform content
- ❐ Academic seminar on various topics
- ❐ Preprofessional or discipline-linked seminar
- ❐ Basic study skills seminar
- ❐ Hybrid
- ❐ Other

You indicated that the first-year seminar type with the highest total enrollment on your campus is [Insert response from Question 22]. Please answer the following questions for only that seminar type.

[To be repeated at the beginning of each page]

23. Please indicate the approximate number of sections of this seminar type that will be offered in the 2012-2013 academic year:

- ❐ 1-10 sections
- ❐ 11-20 sections
- ❐ 21-30 sections
- ❐ 31-40 sections
- ❐ 41-50 sections
- ❐ More than 50 sections

The Students

24. What is the approximate class size for each first-year seminar section?

- ❐ Fewer than 10 students
- ❐ 10-14 students
- ❐ 15-19 students
- ❐ 20-24 students
- ❐ 25-29 students
- ❐ More than 30 students

25. What is the approximate percentage of first-year students *required* to take the first-year seminar?

- ❐ None are required to take it *[Go to Question 27]*
- ❐ Less than 10%
- ❐ 10-19%
- ❐ 20-29%
- ❐ 30-39%
- ❐ 40-49%
- ❐ 50-59%
- ❐ 60-69%
- ❐ 70-79%
- ❐ 80-89%
- ❐ 90-99%
- ❐ 100%

26. Which students, by category, are *required* to take the first-year seminar? (Select all that apply.)

- ❐ All first-year students are required to take it *[Exclusive]*
- ❐ Academically underprepared students
- ❐ First-generation students
- ❐ Honors students
- ❐ International students
- ❐ Learning community participants
- ❐ Preprofessional students (e.g., prelaw, premed)
- ❐ Provisionally admitted students
- ❐ Student athletes
- ❐ Students enrolled in developmental or remedial courses
- ❐ Students participating in dual-enrollment programs
- ❐ Students residing within a particular residence hall
- ❐ Students within specific majors, please list:____________________________
- ❐ Transfer students
- ❐ TRIO participants
- ❐ Undeclared students
- ❐ Other (please specify):____________________________________

27. Please identify unique subpopulations of students for which *special sections* of the first-year seminar are offered: (Select all that apply.)

- ❐ No special sections are offered
- ❐ Academically underprepared students
- ❐ First-generation students
- ❐ Honors students
- ❐ International students
- ❐ Learning community participants
- ❐ Preprofessional students (e.g., prelaw, premed)
- ❐ Provisionally admitted students
- ❐ Student athletes
- ❐ Students enrolled in developmental/remedial courses
- ❐ Students participating in dual-enrollment programs
- ❐ Students residing within a particular residence hall
- ❐ Students within specific majors, please list:______________________________
- ❐ Transfer students
- ❐ TRIO participants
- ❐ Undeclared students
- ❐ Other (please specify)______________________________

The Instructors

28. Who teaches the first-year seminar? (Select all that apply.)

- ❐ Adjunct faculty *[Go to Question 29]*
- ❐ Full-time non-tenure-track faculty *[Go to Question 29]*
- ❐ Tenure-track faculty *[Go to Question 29]*
- ❐ Student affairs professionals *[Go to Question 30]*
- ❐ Other campus professionals (please specify)____________________ *[Go to Question 30]*
- ❐ Graduate students *[Go to Question 31]*
- ❐ Undergraduate students

29. Faculty who teach the first-year seminar teach the course as: (Select all that apply.)

- ❐ Part of regular teaching load
- ❐ An additional course beyond regular teaching load *[Go to Question 32]*
- ❐ Other (please specify)______________________________

30. Staff (student affairs and other campus professionals) who teach the first-year seminar teach the course as: (Select all that apply.)

- ❐ An assigned responsibility
- ❐ An extra responsibility *[Go to Question 32]*
- ❐ Other (please specify)______________________________

31. Graduate students who teach the first-year seminar teach the course as: (Select all that apply.)

- ❒ An assigned responsibility
- ❒ An extra responsibility *[Go to Question 32]*
- ❒ Other (please specify)______________________________

32. If the first-year seminar is taught as an additional course or as an extra responsibility, what type of compensation is offered for teaching a first-year seminar? (Select all that apply.)

- ❒ Direct monetary compensation or stipend *[Go to Question 33]*
- ❒ Graduate student support *[Go to Question 34]*
- ❒ Professional development funds *[Go to Question 35]*
- ❒ Release time *[Go to Question 36]*
- ❒ No additional compensation *[Go to Question 37]*
- ❒ Other (please specify)______________________________

33. Please indicate the amount of direct monetary compensation or stipend: $____________________

34. Please indicate the number of hours per week of graduate student support: ______________hours/week

35. Please indicate the amount of professional development funds: $____________________

36. Please indicate the amount of release time: ____________________credit hours

37. Is instructor training *offered* for first-year seminar instructors?

- ❒ Yes
- ❒ No *[Go to Question 41]*
- ❒ I don't know

38. Is instructor training *required* for first-year seminar instructors?

- ❒ Yes
- ❒ No
- ❒ I don't know

39. How long is the initial instructor training?

- ❒ Half a day or less
- ❒ 1 day
- ❒ 2 days
- ❒ 3 days
- ❒ 4 days
- ❒ 1 week
- ❒ 2 weeks
- ❒ Other (please specify)______________________________

40. Is there ongoing instructor development after initial training?

- ❒ Yes (please describe)______________________________
- ❒ No

41. If undergraduate students assist in the first-year seminar, what is their primary role? (Select all that apply.)

- ❒ They teach independently.
- ❒ They teach as a part of a team.
- ❒ They assist the instructor but do not teach.
- ❒ Other (please specify)____
- ❒ Undergraduate students do not assist in the seminar.

42. Indicate the approximate percentage of sections that are team taught:

- ❒ No sections are team taught. *[Go to Question 44]*
- ❒ Less than 10%
- ❒ 10-19%
- ❒ 20-29%
- ❒ 30-39%
- ❒ 40-49%
- ❒ 50-59%
- ❒ 60-69%
- ❒ 70-79%
- ❒ 80-89%
- ❒ 90-99%
- ❒ 100%

43. Please describe the team configurations (e.g., two faculty, one faculty and one advisor) in your first-year seminar courses:____

44. What is the approximate percentage of students placed in sections with their academic advisors?

- ❒ No students are placed in sections with their academic advisors
- ❒ Less than 10%
- ❒ 10-19%
- ❒ 20-29%
- ❒ 30-39%
- ❒ 40-49%
- ❒ 50-59%
- ❒ 60-69%
- ❒ 70-79%
- ❒ 80-89%
- ❒ 90-99%
- ❒ 100%
- ❒ I don't know

The Course

45. What is the typical duration of a section of the first-year seminar?

- ❒ Half a term
- ❒ One quarter
- ❒ One semester
- ❒ One year
- ❒ Other (please specify)________________________________

46. How many total classroom contact hours are there *per week* in the first-year seminar?

- ❒ 1 hour
- ❒ 2 hours
- ❒ 3 hours
- ❒ 4 hours
- ❒ 5 hours
- ❒ 6 or more hours

47. Does the first-year seminar carry academic credit?

- ❒ Yes
- ❒ No *[Go to Question 50]*
- ❒ I don't know

48. How many credits does the first-year seminar carry?

- ❒ 1 credit
- ❒ 2 credits
- ❒ 3 credits
- ❒ 4 credits
- ❒ 5 credits
- ❒ 6 or more credits

49. How is the first-year seminar credit applied? (Select all that apply.)

- ❒ As an elective
- ❒ Toward general education requirements
- ❒ Toward major requirements
- ❒ Other (please specify)________________________________

50. How is the first-year seminar graded?

- ❒ Letter grade
- ❒ Pass/fail
- ❒ No grade
- ❒ Other (please specify)________________________________

51. Do any sections incorporate online components?

- ❐ Yes
- ❐ No *[Go to Question 54]*
- ❐ I don't know

52. Please describe the online components that are included in the course: ______________________
____
____

53. Are there any online-only sections?

- ❐ Yes
- ❐ No *[Go to Question 55]*
- ❐ I don't know

54. Please indicate the approximate percentage of online-only sections:

- ❐ Less than 10%
- ❐ 10-19%
- ❐ 20-29%
- ❐ 30-39%
- ❐ 40-49%
- ❐ 50-59%
- ❐ 60-69%
- ❐ 70-79%
- ❐ 80-89%
- ❐ 90-99%
- ❐ 100%

55. Select the *three* most important *course objectives* for the first-year seminar:

- ❒ Create common first-year experience
- ❒ Develop a connection with the institution
- ❒ Develop academic skills
- ❒ Develop critical-thinking skills
- ❒ Develop financial literacy
- ❒ Develop information literacy
- ❒ Develop oral communication skills
- ❒ Develop study skills
- ❒ Develop support network or friendships
- ❒ Develop writing skills
- ❒ Develop intercultural competence
- ❒ Improve second-year return rates
- ❒ Increase student-faculty interaction
- ❒ Introduce a discipline
- ❒ Introduce the liberal arts
- ❒ Provide orientation to campus resources and services
- ❒ Provide career exploration
- ❒ Provide preprofessional preparation
- ❒ Self-exploration or personal development
- ❒ Other (please specify)________________________________

56. Select the *three* most important *topics* that compose the content of this first-year seminar:

- ❒ Academic planning or advising
- ❒ Career exploration or preparation
- ❒ Campus engagement
- ❒ Campus resources
- ❒ College policies and procedures
- ❒ Critical thinking
- ❒ Diversity issues
- ❒ Financial literacy
- ❒ Global learning
- ❒ Health and wellness
- ❒ Information literacy
- ❒ Oral communication skills
- ❒ Relationship issues (e.g., interpersonal skills, conflict resolution)
- ❒ Specific disciplinary topic

- ❒ Study skills
- ❒ Time management
- ❒ Writing skills
- ❒ Other (please specify)____________________________

High-Impact Educational Practices

57. Which of the following approaches associated with high-impact educational practices are intentionally incorporated into the first-year seminar? (Select all that apply.)

- ❒ Educational experiences that develop students' ability to produce and revise various forms of writing *[Go to Question 58]*
- ❒ Educational experiences that require collaboration and teamwork with other students *[Go to Question 59]*
- ❒ Educational experiences inside or outside the classroom that help students explore cultures, life experiences, and worldviews different from their own *[Go to Question 59]*

58. Briefly describe up to *three* assignments or activities used to promote the development of writing skills in the seminar:

- ❒ ____________________________
- ❒ ____________________________
- ❒ ____________________________

59. Which of the following high-impact educational practices are connected to the first-year seminar with the highest enrollment of students? (Select all that apply.)

- ❒ **Service-Learning**—Nonremunerative service as part of a course *[Go to Questions 60, 61, 62]*
- ❒ **Learning Community**—Linking a cohort of students in the first-year seminar to one or more other courses or to a common set of theme-based experiences *[Go to Questions 63, 64]*
- ❒ **Common Reading Experience**—First-year reading experience or summer reading program *[Go to Question 65]*
- ❒ **Undergraduate Research**—Scientific inquiry, creative activity, or scholarship guided by a mentor from the faculty or research staff *[Go to Question 66]*

60. How many total hours are students required to complete for the service-learning component?

- ❒ There is no requirement about the total number of hours.
- ❒ 5 or fewer
- ❒ 6-10
- ❒ 11-15
- ❒ 16-20
- ❒ More than 20

61. Which of the following are used as reflection techniques in the first-year seminar associated with the service-learning component? (Select all that apply.)

- ❒ Class discussion
- ❒ Portfolio
- ❒ Student presentations
- ❒ Writing exercise, such as writing a paper or journaling
- ❒ Other (please describe) ____________________
- ❒ There is no reflection associated with the service-learning component.

62. Please describe how sections of the first-year seminar incorporate service-learning: ____________________

____

____

63. Which of the following are characteristics of the learning community of which the first-year seminar is a part? (Select all that apply.)

- ❒ Students are co-enrolled in the first-year seminar and one or more other courses but not all courses in the students' schedules.
- ❒ Students are co-enrolled in the first-year seminar and all other courses in the students' schedules.
- ❒ Course content is intentionally coordinated by the instructors of the first-year seminar and other linked courses.
- ❒ Course content in the first-year seminar and other linked courses is connected by a common intellectual theme.
- ❒ Students in the first-year seminar participate in a common set of theme-based experiences outside of the course, such as discussion groups, a speaker series, or other educational programs.
- ❒ The learning community includes a residential component (i.e., a living-learning community).
- ❒ Other (please describe) ____________________

64. Please describe the role the learning community plays in the first-year seminar: ____________________

____

____

65. Please describe how sections of the first-year seminar incorporate the common reading experience: ____

____

____

66. Please describe how sections of the first-year seminar incorporate undergraduate research: ____________

____

____

The Administration

67. What campus unit directly administers the first-year seminar?

- ❒ Academic affairs central office
- ❒ College or school (e.g., College of Liberal Arts)
- ❒ Academic department(s) (please list)________________
- ❒ First-year program office *[Go to Question 68]*
- ❒ Student affairs central office
- ❒ Other (please specify)________________

68. Which of the following best describes the institutional division where the first-year program office is housed?

- ❒ Academic affairs
- ❒ Student affairs
- ❒ Enrollment management
- ❒ Other (please specify)________________

69. Is there a dean, director, or coordinator of the first-year seminar?

- ❒ Yes
- ❒ No *[Go to Question 73]*
- ❒ I don't know *[Go to Question 73]*

70. Does the dean, director, or coordinator of the first-year seminar work full time or less than full time in this position?

- ❒ Full time (approximately 40 hours per week) *[Go to Question 73]*
- ❒ Less than full time

71. Does the dean, director, or coordinator have another position on campus?

- ❒ Yes
- ❒ No *[Go to Question 73]*
- ❒ I don't know *[Go to Question 73]*

72. The dean, director, or coordinator's other campus role is as a/an: (Select all that apply.)

- ❒ Academic affairs administrator
- ❒ Faculty member
- ❒ Student affairs administrator
- ❒ Other (please specify)________________

Assessment and Evaluation

73. Has your first-year seminar been formally assessed or evaluated since Fall 2009?

- ❒ Yes
- ❒ No *[Go to Question 80]*
- ❒ I don't know *[Go to Question 80]*

74. What type of assessment was conducted? (Select all that apply.)

- ❒ Analysis of institutional data (e.g., GPA, retention rates, graduation) *[Go to Question 78]*
- ❒ Direct assessment of student learning outcomes *[Go to Question 78]*
- ❒ Focus groups with instructors *[Go to Question 78]*
- ❒ Focus groups with students *[Go to Question 78]*
- ❒ Individual interviews with instructors *[Go to Question 78]*
- ❒ Individual interviews with students *[Go to Question 78]*
- ❒ Program review *[Go to Question 78]*
- ❒ Student course evaluation *[Go to Question 78]*
- ❒ Survey instrument *[Go to Question 75]*

75. What type of survey instrument did your institution use to assess or evaluate the first-year seminar? (Select all that apply.)

- ❒ A locally developed (i.e., home-grown) survey of instructors
- ❒ A locally developed survey of students
- ❒ A national survey (e.g., NSSE, CCSSE, CIRP, EBI) *[Go to Question 76]*
- ❒ I don't know

76. Please identify the national survey(s) used to evaluate the first-year seminar. (Select all that apply.)

- ❒ Beginning College Survey of Student Engagement (BCSSE)
- ❒ College Student Experiences Questionnaire (CSEQ)
- ❒ Collegiate Learning Assessment (CLA)
- ❒ Community College Survey of Student Engagement (CCSSE)
- ❒ Cooperative Institutional Research Program (CIRP) Freshman Survey
- ❒ Cooperative Institutional Research Program (CIRP) Your First College Year (YFCY) Survey
- ❒ Faculty Survey of Student Engagement (FSSE)
- ❒ First-Year Initiative (FYI)
- ❒ Individual Developmental and Educational Assessment (IDEA)
- ❒ National Survey of Student Engagement (NSSE)
- ❒ Student Satisfaction Inventory (SSI)
- ❒ Survey of Entering Student Engagement (SENSE)
- ❒ Other (please specify)____________________

77. Please describe any other types of assessment or evaluation processes that were conducted: ___________
____
____

78. Select each student outcome that was measured: (Select all that apply.)

- ❒ Achievement of learning or course outcomes
- ❒ Civic engagement
- ❒ Connections with peers
- ❒ Critical thinking
- ❒ Grade point average
- ❒ Information literacy
- ❒ Involvement in service
- ❒ Out-of-class student-faculty interaction
- ❒ Participation in campus activities
- ❒ Persistence to graduation
- ❒ Persistence to second year
- ❒ Satisfaction with advising
- ❒ Satisfaction with faculty
- ❒ Satisfaction with the seminar
- ❒ Satisfaction with the institution
- ❒ Student self-reports of course impact
- ❒ Student self-reports of improvement
- ❒ Understanding of institutional identity and culture
- ❒ Use of campus services
- ❒ Writing ability
- ❒ Other (please specify)_______________________________

79. Please select the *three* most significant *findings* from your assessment and evaluation of first-year seminar outcomes:

- ❒ _______________________________
- ❒ _______________________________
- ❒ _______________________________

80. It is our practice to make available specific and general information gathered from this survey. In general, findings from the survey are reported in aggregate, but we may identify individual institutions that have agreed to allow their responses to be shared. Please select the appropriate response:

- ❒ You may share my school's name and survey responses.
- ❒ Please do not share my school's name, but you may share my survey responses.
- ❒ Please do not share my survey responses.

81. It is our practice to create a research report based on an analysis of the general information gathered from this survey. Would you like to be informed when this research report is made available?

- ❒ Yes
- ❒ No

82. Beginning with the 2012-13 National Survey of First-Year Seminars, the National Resource Center for The First-Year Experience and Students in Transition will be conducting its national surveys on a four-year cycle. This includes the administration of the National Survey of Sophomore-Year Initiatives in spring 2014 and the National Survey of Senior Capstone Experiences in Spring 2016. More information about these national surveys can be found at *http://www.sc.edu/fye/research/surveys/survey_instruments/index.html*

The National Resource Center will be conducting the National Survey of Sophomore-Year Initiatives in spring 2014. To ensure the survey will be sent to the individual on your campus who is in the best position to answer questions regarding sophomore-year initiatives, please provide this individual's contact information below:

Name: ____

Title: ____

E-mail address: ____

Appendix C: List of Institutions Participating in the 2012-2013 National Survey of First-Year Seminars[3]

Institution Name	City	State
Albion College	Albion	MI
Alvin Community College	Alvin	TX
American Baptist College	Nashville	TN
American University	Washington	DC
Anderson University	Anderson	IN
Anna Maria College	Paxton	MA
Argosy University-Salt Lake City	Draper	UT
Arkansas State University-Main Campus	Jonesboro	AR
Arkansas State University-Newport	Newport	AR
Auburn University	Auburn	AL
Augustana College	Rock Island	IL
Austin College	Sherman	TX
Babson College	Babson Park	MA
Ball State University	Muncie	IN
Bastyr University	Kenmore	WA
Bay Path College	Longmeadow	MA
Beacon College	Leesburg	FL
Benjamin Franklin Institute of Technology	Boston	MA
Bentley University	Waltham	MA
Berry College	Mount Berry	GA
Black Hills State University	Spearfish	SD
Bloomsburg University of Pennsylvania	Bloomsburg	PA
Bristol Community College	Fall River	MA
California Lutheran University	Thousand Oaks	CA
California State University-Channel Islands	Camarillo	CA

[3]This is a partial list ($n = 309$) of total respondents ($n = 896$). Institutions were provided the opportunity to opt out of being publicly identified as a survey respondent.

Institution Name	City	State
California State University-Fresno	Fresno	CA
California State University-Fullerton	Fullerton	CA
California State University-Monterey Bay	Seaside	CA
California State University-San Bernardino	San Bernardino	CA
Cameron University	Lawton	OK
Campbell University	Buies Creek	NC
Carlow University	Pittsburgh	PA
Carroll College	Helena	MT
Case Western Reserve University	Cleveland	OH
Cayuga County Community College	Auburn	NY
Cazenovia College	Cazenovia	NY
Central College	Pella	IA
Central Community College	Grand Island	NE
Central Connecticut State University	New Britain	CT
Central Washington University	Ellensburg	WA
Chapman University	Orange	CA
Chatham University	Pittsburgh	PA
Chief Dull Knife College	Lame Deer	MT
Citadel Military College of South Carolina	Charleston	SC
Clayton State University	Morrow	GA
Clearwater Christian College	Clearwater	FL
Coastline Community College	Fountain Valley	CA
College for Creative Studies	Detroit	MI
College of Charleston	Charleston	SC
College of Saint Benedict	Saint Joseph	MN
Columbus College of Art and Design	Columbus	OH
Crossroads Bible College	Indianapolis	IN
CUNY Brooklyn College	Brooklyn	NY
CUNY John Jay College of Criminal Justice	New York	NY
Cuyamaca College	Rancho San Diego	CA
D'Youville College	Buffalo	NY
Dalton State College	Dalton	GA
DeVry University's Keller Graduate School of Management-Virginia	Arlington	VA
Dixie State College of Utah	St. George	UT
Dominican College of Blauvelt	Orangeburg	NY
Drake University	Des Moines	IA
Drury University	Springfield	MO
Durham Technical Community College	Durham	NC
East Carolina University	Greenville	NC
East Los Angeles College	Monterey Park	CA
Eastern New Mexico University-Main Campus	Portales	NM
Edgewood College	Madison	WI

Institution Name	City	State
Edison State Community College	Piqua	OH
Elizabeth City State University	Elizabeth City	NC
Elmhurst College	Elmhurst	IL
Emmanuel College	Boston	MA
Eureka College	Eureka	IL
Fayetteville State University	Fayetteville	NC
Ferris State University	Big Rapids	MI
Florida Gulf Coast University	Fort Myers	FL
Florida Institute of Technology	Melbourne	FL
Framingham State University	Framingham	MA
Franklin College	Franklin	IA
Franklin W. Olin College of Engineering	Needham	MA
Frostburg State University	Frostburg	MD
Genesee Community College	Batavia	NY
Georgia College & State University	Milledgeville	GA
Georgia Gwinnett College	Lawrenceville	GA
Georgia Southern University	Statesboro	GA
Georgian Court University	Lakewood	NJ
Gettysburg College	Gettysburg	PA
Gogebic Community College	Ironwood	MI
Grand Rapids Community College	Grand Rapids	MI
Grand View University	Des Moines	IA
Grossmont College	El Cajon	CA
Gustavus Adolphus College	St. Peter	MN
Hannibal-LaGrange University	Hannibal	MO
Harper College	Palatine	IL
Heidelberg University	Tiffin	OH
Hesston College	Hesston	KS
Hiram College	Hiram	OH
Holy Names University	Oakland	CA
Horry-Georgetown Technical College	Conway	SC
Houston Baptist University	Houston	TX
Humboldt State University	Arcata	CA
Husson University	Bangor	ME
Indiana University-Purdue University-Indianapolis	Indianapolis	IN
Indiana University-Southeast	New Albany	IN
Jackson Community College	Jackson	MI
James A. Rhodes State College	Lima	OH
Jamestown Community College	Jamestown	NY
Jefferson Community and Technical College	Louisville	KY
Johnson & Wales University-Providence	Providence	RI
Johnson College	Scranton	PA
Juniata College	Huntingdon	PA

Institution Name	City	State
Kalamazoo College	Kalamazoo	MI
Kennesaw State University	Kennesaw	GA
Kent State University at Stark	North Canton	OH
Keystone College	La Plume	PA
La Roche College	Pittsburgh	PA
La Salle University	Philadelphia	PA
Lafayette College	Easton	PA
LaGrange College	LaGrange	GA
Lasell College	Newton	MA
Lehigh University	Bethlehem	PA
Limestone College	Gaffney	SC
Lindsey Wilson College	Columbia	KY
Longwood University	Farmville	VA
Loras College	Dubuque	IA
Louisiana State University and Agricultural & Mechanical College	Baton Rouge	LA
Lourdes University	Sylvania	OH
Loyola Marymount University	Los Angeles	CA
Loyola University Maryland	Baltimore	MD
Lycoming College	Williamsport	PA
Lynn University	Boca Raton	FL
Macalester College	St. Paul	MN
Macomb Community College	Warren	MI
Madonna University	Livonia	MI
Manchester Community College	Manchester	NH
Manchester University	North Manchester	IN
Marshall University	Huntington	WV
Maryville College	Maryville	TN
Massachusetts Bay Community College	Wellesley Hills	MA
Massachusetts Institute of Technology	Cambridge	MA
McKendree University	Lebanon	IL
McLennan Community College	Waco	TX
Menlo College	Atherton	CA
Mercy College of Health Sciences	Des Moines	IA
Methodist University	Fayetteville	NC
Mid-Continent University	Mayfield	KY
Middlesex Community College	Bedford/Lowell	MA
Miles Community College	Miles City	MT
Milwaukee School of Engineering	Milwaukee	WI
Minnesota State University-Mankato	Mankato	MN
MiraCosta College	Oceanside	CA
Missouri State University-Springfield	Springfield	MO
Monroe Community College	Rochester	NY

Institution Name	City	State
Montcalm Community College	Sidney	MI
Montclair State University	Montclair	NJ
Moody Bible Institute	Chicago	IL
Morningside College	Sioux City	IA
Mount St. Mary's University	Emmitsburg	MD
Murray State University	Murray	KY
Nash Community College	Rocky Mount	NC
Nassau Community College	Garden City	NY
New Mexico Military Institute	Roswell	NM
Newman University	Wichita	KS
Niagara University	Niagara University	NY
Nichols College	Dudley	MA
North Georgia College & State University	Dahlonega	GA
North Park University	Chicago	IL
Northern Illinois University	DeKalb	IL
Northland Community and Technical College	East Grand Forks	MN
Norwich University	Northfield	VT
Ohio State University-Newark Campus	Newark	OH
Ohio University-Main Campus	Athens	OH
Ohio University-Southern Campus	Ironton	OH
Oklahoma City University	Oklahoma City	OK
Onondaga Community College	Syracuse	NY
Orangeburg Calhoun Technical College	Orangeburg	SC
Pacific Lutheran University	Tacoma	WA
Paradise Valley Community College	Phoenix	AZ
Parkland College	Champaign	IL
Pasadena City College	Pasadena	CA
Pennsylvania State University Mont Alto	Mont Alto	PA
Philadelphia University	Philadelphia	PA
Piedmont Virginia Community College	Charlottesville	VA
Point Park University	Pittsburgh	PA
Prince George's Community College	Largo	MD
Radford University	Radford	VA
Regent University	Virginia Beach	VA
Regis College	Weston	MA
Roosevelt University	Chicago	IL
Saint Cloud State University	Saint Cloud	MN
Saint Gregory's University	Shawnee	OK
Saint John's University	Collegeville	MN
Saint Joseph's College	Rensselaer	IN
Saint Leo University	Saint Leo	FL
Saint Martin's University	Lacey	WA
Saint Michael's College	Colchester	VT

Institution Name	City	State
Salt Lake Community College	Salt Lake City	UT
Samford University	Birmingham	AL
San Francisco Art Institute	San Francisco	CA
Santa Ana College	Santa Ana	CA
Santa Clara University	Santa Clara	CA
Seattle Pacific University	Seattle	WA
Seton Hall University	South Orange	NJ
Shepherd University	Shepherdstown	WV
Sinclair Community College	Dayton	OH
Sitting Bull College	Fort Yates	ND
Smith College	Northampton	MA
South Mountain Community College	Phoenix	AZ
Southeast Arkansas College	Pine Bluff	AR
Southern Nazarene University	Bethany	OK
Southern Oregon University	Ashland	OR
Southwestern College	Chula Vista	CA
Southwestern University	Georgetown	TX
Spartanburg Methodist College	Spartanburg	SC
Spencerian College-Lexington	Lexington	KY
Spring Arbor University	Spring Arbor	MI
St. Cloud Technical and Community College	St. Cloud	MN
St. Mary's College of Maryland	St. Mary's City	MD
St. Philip's College	San Antonio	TX
Stephen F. Austin State University	Nacogdoches	TX
Stetson University	DeLand	FL
SUNY College at Brockport	Brockport	NY
SUNY College at Cortland	Cortland	NY
SUNY College at Old Westbury	Old Westbury	NY
SUNY College at Plattsburgh	Plattsburgh	NY
Susquehanna University	Selinsgrove	PA
Syracuse University	Syracuse	NY
Tennessee Wesleyan College	Athens	TN
Texas A & M University-College Station	College Station	TX
Texas A & M University-Kingsville	Kingsville	TX
Texas State Technical College-West Texas	Sweetwater	TX
The College of Saint Scholastica	Duluth	MN
The Richard Stockton College of New Jersey	Galloway	NJ
The University of Alabama	Tuscaloosa	AL
The University of Tampa	Tampa	FL
The University of Texas at Arlington	Arlington	TX
The University of Texas at El Paso	El Paso	TX
The University of Texas-Pan American	Edinburg	TX
Thomas College	Waterville	ME

Institution Name	City	State
Three Rivers Community College	Norwich	CT
Transylvania University	Lexington	KY
Tri-County Technical College	Pendleton	SC
Trident Technical College	Charleston,	SC
Tulsa Community College	Tulsa	OK
Union County College	Cranford	NJ
Universidad Metropolitana	San Juan	PR
University at Buffalo	Buffalo	NY
University of Akron Wayne College	Orrville	OH
University of Arizona	Tucson	AZ
University of California-Berkeley	Berkeley	CA
University of California-Davis	Davis	CA
University of Central Oklahoma	Edmond	OK
University of Cincinnati-Main Campus	Cincinnati	OH
University of Hartford	West Hartford	CT
University of Houston	Houston	TX
University of Idaho	Moscow	ID
University of Illinois at Springfield	Springfield	IL
University of La Verne	La Verne	CA
University of Louisiana-Monroe	Monroe	LA
University of Mary	Bismarck	ND
University of Massachusetts-Lowell	Lowell	MA
University of Michigan-Ann Arbor	Ann Arbor	MI
University of Minnesota-Crookston	Crookston	MN
University of Mississippi	University	MS
University of New Mexico-Gallup Campus	Gallup	NM
University of New Mexico-Main Campus	Albuquerque	NM
University of North Carolina at Chapel Hill	Chapel Hill	NC
University of North Carolina at Charlotte	Charlotte	NC
University of North Carolina at Wilmington	Wilmington	NC
University of North Texas	Denton	TX
University of Rhode Island	Kingston	RI
University of Sacred Heart	Santurce	PR
University of South Carolina-Columbia	Columbia	SC
University of the Cumberlands	Williamsburg	KY
University of the Pacific	Stockton	CA
University of Toledo	Toledo	OH
University of Wisconsin Colleges	Madison	WI
University of Wisconsin-La Crosse	La Crosse	WI
University of Wisconsin-Superior	Superior	WI
University of Wyoming	Laramie	WY
Ursinus College	Collegeville	PA
Valencia College	Orlando	FL

Institution Name	City	State
Vance-Granville Community College	Henderson	NC
Vanderbilt University	Nashville	TN
Vassar College	Poughkeepsie	NY
Villanova University	Villanova	PA
Virginia Highlands Community College	Abingdon	VA
Virginia Military Institute	Lexington	VA
Wabash College	Crawfordsville	IN
Waldorf College Forest City	Forest City	IA
Walsh University	North Canton	OH
Warner University	Lake Wales	FL
Wartburg College	Waverly	IA
Washington State University	Pullman	WA
Wayne Community College	Goldsboro	NC
Weatherford College	Weatherford	TX
Wentworth Institute of Technology	Boston	MA
West Valley College	Saratoga	CA
West Virginia University	Morgantown	WV
West Virginia Wesleyan College	Buckhannon	WV
Western Kentucky University	Bowling Green	KY
Western Michigan University	Kalamazoo	MI
Western Nebraska Community College	Scottsbluff	NE
Western New England University	Springfield	MA
Western Washington University	Bellinghham	WA
William Paterson University of New Jersey	Wayne	NJ
Winona State University	Winona	MN
Wor-Wic Community College	Salisbury	MD
Worcester Polytechnic Institute	Worcester	MA
Worcester State University	Worcester	MA

Appendix D: Response Frequencies 2012-2013 National Survey of First-Year Seminars

All Responses by Instituitional Type, Control, and Size

	Institution type				Institution control				Number of entering first-year students											
	Two-year		Four-year		Public		Private		Less than 500		501-1,000		1,001-2,000		2,001-4,000		More than 4,000		Total	
Survey question/responses	Freq.	%	Freq.	%	Freq.	%	Freq.	%	Freq.	%	Freq.	%	Freq.	%	Freq.	%	Freq.	%	Freq.	%
Q12. Does your institution, including any department or division, currently offer one or more first-year seminars?																				
Yes	206	86.2	598	91.0	438	90.3	366	89.1	237	88.8	182	89.2	156	89.7	132	91.7	97	90.7	804	89.7
No	33	13.8	56	8.5	47	9.7	42	10.2	28	10.5	21	10.3	18	10.3	12	8.3	10	9.3	89	9.9
I don't know	0	0.0	3	0.5	0	0.0	3	0.7	2	0.7	1	0.5	0	0.0	0	0.0	0	0.0	3	0.3
Total	239	100.0	657	100.0	485	100.0	411	100.0	267	100.0	204	100.0	174	100.0	144	100.0	107	100.0	896	100.0
Q13. Has your institution ever offered one or more first-year seminars?																				
Yes	8	25.0	26	44.8	19	42.2	15	33.3	12	40.0	6	30.0	5	27.8	5	41.7	6	60.0	34	37.8
No	20	62.5	28	48.3	21	46.7	27	60.0	16	53.3	12	60.0	10	55.6	7	58.3	3	30.0	48	53.3
I don't know	4	12.5	4	6.9	5	11.1	3	6.7	2	6.7	2	10.0	3	16.7	0	0.0	1	10.0	8	8.9
Total	32	100.0	58	100.0	45	100.0	45	100.0	30	100.0	20	100.0	18	100.0	12	100.0	10	100.0	90	100.0
Q14. Why does your institution not currently offer a first-year seminar?																				
First-year issues are not an institutional priority	2	6.3	8	13.8	3	6.7	7	15.6	4	13.3	3	15.0	1	5.6	1	8.3	1	10.0	10	11.1
Lack of expertise	3	9.4	2	3.4	3	6.7	2	4.4	2	6.7	1	5.0	1	5.6	1	8.3	0	0.0	5	5.6
Lack of funding	17	53.1	17	29.3	25	55.6	9	20.0	6	20.0	6	30.0	10	55.6	8	66.7	4	40.0	34	37.8
Lack of staff or faculty buy-in	11	34.4	21	36.2	15	33.3	17	37.8	12	40.0	6	30.0	6	33.3	4	33.3	4	40.0	32	35.6
Limited time	12	37.5	6	10.3	13	28.9	5	11.1	2	6.7	4	20.0	6	33.3	4	33.3	2	20.0	18	20.0
Other (please specify)	12	37.5	30	51.7	14	31.1	28	62.2	17	56.7	10	50.0	7	38.9	4	33.3	4	40.0	42	46.7
Total	32	100.0	58	100.0	45	100.0	45	100.0	30	100.0	20	100.0	18	100.0	12	100.0	10	100.0	90	100.0

Table continues p. 86

Table continued from pg. 85

	Institution type				Institution control				Number of entering first-year students										Total	
	Two-year		Four-year		Public		Private		Less than 500		501-1,000		1,001-2,000		2,001-4,000		More than 4,000			
Survey question/responses	Freq.	%	Freq.	%	Freq.	%	Freq.	%	Freq.	%	Freq.	%	Freq.	%	Freq.	%	Freq.	%	Freq.	%
Q15. Is your institution considering or developing a first-year seminar?																				
Yes	20	62.5	28	48.3	31	68.9	17	37.8	10	33.3	11	55.0	10	55.6	10	83.3	7	70.0	48	53.3
No	11	34.4	24	41.4	13	28.9	22	48.9	16	53.3	8	40.0	7	38.9	1	8.3	3	30.0	35	38.9
I don't know	1	3.1	6	10.3	1	2.2	6	13.3	4	13.3	1	5.0	1	5.6	1	8.3	0	0.0	7	7.8
Total	32	100.0	58	100.0	45	100.0	45	100.0	30	100.0	20	100.0	18	100.0	12	100.0	10	100.0	90	100.0
Q16. Which of the following high-impact educational practices does your institution offer for first-year students?																				
Common reading experience	4	12.5	25	43.1	10	22.2	19	42.2	9	30.0	7	35.0	6	33.3	3	25.0	4	40.0	29	32.2
Learning community	9	28.1	25	43.1	19	42.2	15	33.3	6	20.0	7	35.0	8	44.4	7	58.3	6	60.0	34	37.8
Service -learning	11	34.4	25	43.1	19	42.2	17	37.8	9	30.0	9	45.0	8	44.4	4	33.3	6	60.0	36	40.0
Undergraduate research	1	3.1	20	34.5	11	24.4	10	22.2	6	20.0	3	15.0	7	38.9	2	16.7	3	30.0	21	23.3
None of the above	15	46.9	16	27.6	15	33.3	16	35.6	15	50.0	7	35.0	3	16.7	5	41.7	1	10.0	31	34.4
Total	32	100.0	58	100.0	45	100.0	45	100.0	30	100.0	20	100.0	18	100.0	12	100.0	10	100.0	90	100.0
Q17. What is the approximate percentage of first-year students who take a first-year seminar on your campus?																				
Less than 10%	33	16.3	18	3.1	49	11.4	2	0.6	7	3.0	9	5.0	10	6.5	12	9.4	13	13.7	51	6.4
10-19%	23	11.3	25	4.2	43	10.0	5	1.4	7	3.0	8	4.4	11	7.1	10	7.8	12	12.6	48	6.1
20-29%	18	8.9	29	4.9	37	8.6	10	2.8	2	0.9	12	6.6	12	7.7	13	10.2	8	8.4	47	5.9
30-39%	16	7.9	19	3.2	31	7.2	4	1.1	4	1.7	0	0.0	8	5.2	12	9.4	11	11.6	35	4.4
40-49%	8	3.9	22	3.7	25	5.8	5	1.4	3	1.3	6	3.3	4	2.6	10	7.8	7	7.4	30	3.8
50-59%	21	10.3	17	2.9	32	7.4	6	1.7	7	3.0	8	4.4	11	7.1	6	4.7	6	6.3	38	4.8
60-69%	13	6.4	15	2.5	22	5.1	6	1.7	2	0.9	7	3.9	8	5.2	7	5.5	4	4.2	28	3.5
70-79%	21	10.3	25	4.2	38	8.8	8	2.2	6	2.6	12	6.6	12	7.7	9	7.0	7	7.4	46	5.8
80-89%	17	8.4	33	5.6	36	8.4	14	3.9	9	3.9	14	7.7	9	5.8	12	9.4	6	6.3	50	6.3
90-99%	24	11.8	125	21.2	67	15.6	82	22.7	53	22.7	35	19.3	29	18.7	20	15.6	12	12.6	149	18.8
100%	9	4.4	261	44.3	50	11.6	220	60.8	133	57.1	70	38.7	41	26.5	17	13.3	9	9.5	270	34.1
Total	203	100.0	589	100.0	430	100.0	362	100.0	233	100.0	181	100.0	155	100.0	128	100.0	95	100.0	792	100.0

	Institution type				Institution control				Number of entering first-year students										Total	
	Two-year		Four-year		Public		Private		Less than 500		501-1,000		1,001-2,000		2,001-4,000		More than 4,000			
Survey question/responses	Freq.	%	Freq.	%	Freq.	%	Freq.	%	Freq.	%	Freq.	%	Freq.	%	Freq.	%	Freq.	%	Freq.	%
Q18. Approximately how many years has a first-year seminar been offered on your campus?																				
2 years or less	31	15.3	33	5.6	46	10.7	18	5.0	16	6.9	15	8.3	12	7.7	10	7.8	11	11.6	64	8.1
3-5 years	58	28.6	80	13.6	85	19.8	53	14.6	42	18.0	31	17.1	30	19.4	22	17.2	13	13.7	138	17.4
6-10 years	53	26.1	147	25.0	113	26.3	87	24.0	54	23.2	48	26.5	42	27.1	35	27.3	21	22.1	200	25.3
11-15 years	28	13.8	114	19.4	78	18.1	64	17.7	44	18.9	27	14.9	28	18.1	24	18.8	19	20.0	142	17.9
16-20 years	12	5.9	97	16.5	48	11.2	61	16.9	30	12.9	32	17.7	19	12.3	17	13.3	11	11.6	109	13.8
More than 20 years	21	10.3	118	20.0	60	14.0	79	21.8	47	20.2	28	15.5	24	15.5	20	15.6	20	21.1	139	17.6
Total	203	100.0	589	100.0	430	100.0	362	100.0	233	100.0	181	100.0	155	100.0	128	100.0	95	100.0	792	100.0
Q19. Which of the following types of first-year seminars does your institution currently offer?																				
Extended orientation seminar	151	75.1	325	55.4	288	67.4	188	52.1	127	54.7	108	59.7	90	58.4	87	68.5	64	68.1	476	60.4
Academic seminar - uniform content	52	25.9	180	30.7	117	27.4	115	31.9	74	31.9	52	28.7	39	25.3	37	29.1	30	31.9	232	29.4
Academic seminar - various topics	18	9.0	208	35.4	102	23.9	124	34.3	57	24.6	56	30.9	45	29.2	36	28.3	32	34.0	226	28.7
Preprofessional or discipline-linked seminar	19	9.5	110	18.7	97	22.7	32	8.9	13	5.6	27	14.9	20	13.0	33	26.0	36	38.3	129	16.4
Basic study skills seminar	71	35.3	107	18.2	118	27.6	60	16.6	41	17.7	34	18.8	30	19.5	45	35.4	28	29.8	178	22.6
Hybrid	31	15.4	153	26.1	100	23.4	84	23.3	57	24.6	42	23.2	36	23.4	30	23.6	19	20.2	184	23.4
Other	2	1.0	10	1.7	8	1.9	4	1.1	2	0.9	2	1.1	4	2.6	2	1.6	2	2.1	12	1.5
Total	201	100.0	587	100.0	427	100.0	361	100.0	232	100.0	181	100.0	154	100.0	127	100.0	94	100.0	788	100.0

Table continues p. 88

Table continued from p. 87

	Institution type				Institution control				Number of entering first-year students										Total	
	Two-year		Four-year		Public		Private		Less than 500		501-1,000		1,001-2,000		2,001-4,000		More than 4,000			
Survey question/responses	Freq.	%	Freq.	%	Freq.	%	Freq.	%	Freq.	%	Freq.	%	Freq.	%	Freq.	%	Freq.	%	Freq.	%
Q22. Which of the following first-year seminars has the highest student enrollment at your institution?																				
Extended orientation seminar	108	54.0	199	34.0	202	47.4	105	29.2	82	35.3	63	35.0	60	39.0	62	48.8	40	43.0	307	39.1
Academic seminar - uniform content	41	20.5	108	18.4	74	17.4	75	20.8	51	22.0	36	20.0	28	18.2	20	15.7	14	15.1	149	19.0
Academic seminar - various topics	6	3.0	145	24.7	53	12.4	98	27.2	46	19.8	42	23.3	34	22.1	14	11.0	15	16.1	151	19.2
Preprofessional or discipline-linked seminar	4	2.0	26	4.4	23	5.4	7	1.9	3	1.3	6	3.3	4	2.6	7	5.5	10	10.8	30	3.8
Basic study skills seminar	23	11.5	8	1.4	24	5.6	7	1.9	6	2.6	4	2.2	4	2.6	11	8.7	6	6.5	31	3.9
Hybrid	17	8.5	94	16.0	48	11.3	63	17.5	40	17.2	28	15.6	22	14.3	13	10.2	8	8.6	111	14.1
Other	1	0.5	6	1.0	2	0.5	5	1.4	4	1.7	1	0.6	2	1.3	0	0.0	0	0.0	7	0.9
Total	200	100.0	586	100.0	426	100.0	360	100.0	232	100.0	180	100.0	154	100.0	127	100.0	93	100.0	786	100.0
Q23. Please indicate the approximate number of sections of this seminar type that will be offered in the 2012-2013 academic year:																				
1-10 sections	56	28.0	110	18.8	83	19.5	83	23.1	85	36.6	36	20.0	22	14.3	15	11.8	8	8.6	166	21.1
11-20 sections	48	24.0	140	23.9	80	18.8	108	30.0	86	37.1	37	20.6	27	17.5	26	20.5	12	12.9	188	23.9
21-30 sections	32	16.0	120	20.5	73	17.1	79	21.9	50	21.6	45	25.0	26	16.9	15	11.8	16	17.2	152	19.3
31-40 sections	14	7.0	63	10.8	44	10.3	33	9.2	7	3.0	35	19.4	13	8.4	9	7.1	13	14.0	77	9.8
41-50 sections	19	9.5	44	7.5	41	9.6	22	6.1	4	1.7	20	11.1	14	9.1	18	14.2	7	7.5	63	8.0
More than 50 sections	31	15.5	109	18.6	105	24.6	35	9.7	0	0.0	7	3.9	52	33.8	44	34.6	37	39.8	140	17.8
Total	200	100.0	586	100.0	426	100.0	360	100.0	232	100.0	180	100.0	154	100.0	127	100.0	93	100.0	786	100.0

	Institution type				Institution control				Number of entering first-year students											
	Two-year		Four-year		Public		Private		Less than 500		501-1,000		1,001-2,000		2,001-4,000		More than 4,000		Total	
Survey question/responses	Freq.	%	Freq.	%	Freq.	%	Freq.	%	Freq.	%	Freq.	%	Freq.	%	Freq.	%	Freq.	%	Freq.	%
Q24. What is the approximate class size for each first-year seminar section?																				
Fewer than 10 students	1	0.5	4	0.7	2	0.5	3	0.8	3	1.3	1	0.6	1	0.6	0	0.0	0	0.0	5	0.6
10-14 students	13	6.5	48	8.2	19	4.5	42	11.7	37	15.9	12	6.7	7	4.5	4	3.1	1	1.1	61	7.8
15-19 students	42	21.1	240	41.1	89	21.0	193	53.8	119	51.3	79	44.4	39	25.3	21	16.5	24	26.1	282	36.0
20-24 students	83	41.7	179	30.7	178	42.0	84	23.4	49	21.1	56	31.5	63	40.9	57	44.9	37	40.2	262	33.5
25-29 students	40	20.1	64	11.0	88	20.8	16	4.5	6	2.6	17	9.6	29	18.8	34	26.8	18	19.6	104	13.3
More than 30 students	20	10.1	49	8.4	48	11.3	21	5.8	18	7.8	13	7.3	15	9.7	11	8.7	12	13.0	69	8.8
Total	199	100.0	584	100.0	424	100.0	359	100.0	232	100.0	178	100.0	154	100.0	127	100.0	92	100.0	783	100.0
Q25. What is the approximate percentage of first-year students required to take the first-year seminar?																				
None are required to take it	48	24.1	83	14.2	108	25.5	23	6.4	11	4.7	26	14.6	26	16.9	37	29.1	31	33.7	131	16.7
Less than 10%	14	7.0	26	4.5	34	8.0	6	1.7	5	2.2	9	5.1	7	4.5	11	8.7	8	8.7	40	5.1
10-19%	13	6.5	22	3.8	31	7.3	4	1.1	4	1.7	5	2.8	7	4.5	10	7.9	9	9.8	35	4.5
20-29%	7	3.5	17	2.9	18	4.2	6	1.7	3	1.3	2	1.1	6	3.9	5	3.9	8	8.7	24	3.1
30-39%	6	3.0	9	1.5	15	3.5	0	0.0	3	1.3	1	0.6	4	2.6	4	3.1	3	3.3	15	1.9
40-49%	7	3.5	5	0.9	11	2.6	1	0.3	2	0.9	2	1.1	4	2.6	3	2.4	1	1.1	12	1.5
50-59%	13	6.5	5	0.9	15	3.5	3	0.8	3	1.3	7	3.9	6	3.9	2	1.6	0	0.0	18	2.3
60-69%	9	4.5	4	0.7	11	2.6	2	0.6	2	0.9	0	0.0	6	3.9	2	1.6	3	3.3	13	1.7
70-79%	14	7.0	12	2.1	21	5.0	5	1.4	3	1.3	9	5.1	7	4.5	4	3.1	3	3.3	26	3.3
80-89%	18	9.0	13	2.2	18	4.2	13	3.6	12	5.2	6	3.4	5	3.2	6	4.7	2	2.2	31	4.0
90-99%	20	10.1	85	14.6	44	10.4	61	17.0	40	17.2	27	15.2	15	9.7	15	11.8	8	8.7	105	13.4
100%	30	15.1	303	51.9	98	23.1	235	65.5	144	62.1	84	47.2	61	39.6	28	22.0	16	17.4	333	42.5
Total	199	100.0	584	100.0	424	100.0	359	100.0	232	100.0	178	100.0	154	100.0	127	100.0	92	100.0	783	100.0

Table continues p. 90

Table continued from p. 89

	Institution type				Institution control				Number of entering first-year students										Total	
	Two-year		Four-year		Public		Private		Less than 500		501-1,000		1,001-2,000		2,001-4,000		More than 4,000			
Survey question/responses	**Freq.**	**%**	**Freq.**	**%**	**Freq.**	**%**	**Freq.**	**%**	**Freq.**	**%**	**Freq.**	**%**	**Freq.**	**%**	**Freq.**	**%**	**Freq.**	**%**	**Freq.**	**%**
Q26. Which students, by category, are required to take the first-year seminar?																				
All first-year students are required to take it	64	42.7	375	75.2	147	47.0	292	86.9	190	86.0	112	73.7	74	58.3	43	47.8	20	33.9	439	67.6
Academically underprepared students	42	28.0	39	7.8	71	22.7	10	3.0	13	5.9	15	9.9	17	13.4	21	23.3	15	25.4	81	12.5
First-generation students	6	4.0	10	2.0	10	3.2	6	1.8	4	1.8	3	2.0	2	1.6	4	4.4	3	5.1	16	2.5
Honors students	3	2.0	10	2.0	9	2.9	4	1.2	0	0.0	6	3.9	3	2.4	2	2.2	2	3.4	13	2.0
International students	1	0.7	9	1.8	5	1.6	5	1.5	3	1.4	3	2.0	2	1.6	1	1.1	1	1.7	10	1.5
Learning community participants	8	5.3	23	4.6	25	8.0	6	1.8	4	1.8	6	3.9	6	4.7	5	5.6	10	16.9	31	4.8
Preprofessional students (e.g., prelaw, premed)	2	1.3	12	2.4	8	2.6	6	1.8	1	0.5	4	2.6	1	0.8	2	2.2	6	10.2	14	2.2
Provisionally admitted students	3	2.0	29	5.8	23	7.3	9	2.7	6	2.7	7	4.6	6	4.7	5	5.6	8	13.6	32	4.9
Student athletes	6	4.0	16	3.2	18	5.8	4	1.2	1	0.5	3	2.0	5	3.9	6	6.7	7	11.9	22	3.4
Students enrolled in developmental or remedial courses	31	20.7	15	3.0	39	12.5	7	2.1	7	3.2	8	5.3	15	11.8	10	11.1	6	10.2	46	7.1
Students participating in dual-enrollment programs	2	1.3	1	0.2	2	0.6	1	0.3	1	0.5	1	0.7	1	0.8	0	0.0	0	0.0	3	0.5
Students residing within a particular residence hall	0	0.0	5	1.0	3	1.0	2	0.6	1	0.5	0	0.0	1	0.8	1	1.1	2	3.4	5	0.8
Transfer students	4	2.7	2	0.4	4	1.3	2	0.6	1	0.5	1	0.7	4	3.1	0	0.0	0	0.0	6	0.9
TRIO participants	7	4.7	16	3.2	18	5.8	5	1.5	4	1.8	5	3.3	1	0.8	4	4.4	9	15.3	23	3.5
Undeclared students	0	0.0	17	3.4	13	4.2	4	1.2	2	0.9	1	0.7	3	2.4	5	5.6	6	10.2	17	2.6
Students within specific majors (please specify)	20	13.3	31	6.2	42	13.4	9	2.7	3	1.4	10	6.6	17	13.4	9	10.0	12	20.3	51	7.9
Other (please specify)	24	16.0	41	8.2	46	14.7	19	5.7	12	5.4	13	8.6	16	12.6	15	16.7	9	15.3	65	10.0
Total	150	100.0	499	100.0	313	100.0	336	100.0	221	100.0	152	100.0	127	100.0	90	100.0	59	100.0	649	100.0

	Institution type				Institution control				Number of entering first-year students										Total	
	Two-year		Four-year		Public		Private		Less than 500		501-1,000		1,001-2,000		2,001-4,000		More than 4,000			
Survey question/responses	Freq.	%	Freq.	%	Freq.	%	Freq.	%	Freq.	%	Freq.	%	Freq.	%	Freq.	%	Freq.	%	Freq.	%
Q27. Please identify unique subpopulations of students for which special sections of the first-year seminar are offered.																				
No special sections are offered	92	46.5	213	36.6	148	35.2	157	43.7	120	51.7	70	39.3	56	36.6	39	30.7	20	22.2	305	39.1
Academically underprepared students	35	17.7	95	16.3	75	17.8	55	15.3	30	12.9	29	16.3	19	12.4	30	23.6	22	24.4	130	16.7
First-generation students	6	3.0	35	6.0	29	6.9	12	3.3	4	1.7	14	7.9	6	3.9	7	5.5	10	11.1	41	5.3
Honors students	7	3.5	181	31.1	91	21.6	97	27.0	41	17.7	52	29.2	40	26.1	25	19.7	30	33.3	188	24.1
International students	7	3.5	47	8.1	32	7.6	22	6.1	11	4.7	8	4.5	14	9.2	12	9.4	9	10.0	54	6.9
Learning community participants	33	16.7	115	19.8	112	26.6	36	10.0	19	8.2	34	19.1	28	18.3	34	26.8	33	36.7	148	19.0
Preprofessional students (e.g., prelaw, premed)	5	2.5	55	9.5	45	10.7	15	4.2	8	3.4	15	8.4	5	3.3	13	10.2	19	21.1	60	7.7
Provisionally admitted students	0	0.0	38	6.5	25	5.9	13	3.6	5	2.2	4	2.2	7	4.6	12	9.4	10	11.1	38	4.9
Student athletes	15	7.6	45	7.7	50	11.9	10	2.8	5	2.2	7	3.9	12	7.8	20	15.7	16	17.8	60	7.7
Students enrolled in developmental or remedial courses	22	11.1	24	4.1	38	9.0	8	2.2	5	2.2	8	4.5	13	8.5	14	11.0	6	6.7	46	5.9
Students participating in dual enrollment programs	6	3.0	6	1.0	10	2.4	2	0.6	0	0.0	1	0.6	5	3.3	4	3.1	2	2.2	12	1.5
Students residing within a particular residence hall	0	0.0	29	5.0	22	5.2	7	1.9	4	1.7	6	3.4	4	2.6	5	3.9	10	11.1	29	3.7
Transfer students	6	3.0	52	8.9	30	7.1	28	7.8	19	8.2	8	4.5	8	5.2	11	8.7	12	13.3	58	7.4
TRIO participants	9	4.5	35	6.0	37	8.8	7	1.9	6	2.6	10	5.6	7	4.6	10	7.9	11	12.2	44	5.6
Undeclared students	5	2.5	67	11.5	52	12.4	20	5.6	6	2.6	14	7.9	15	9.8	19	15.0	18	20.0	72	9.2
Students within specific majors (please specify)	18	9.1	93	16.0	81	19.2	30	8.4	14	6.0	18	10.1	29	19.0	27	21.3	23	25.6	111	14.2
Other (please specify)	23	11.6	61	10.5	64	15.2	20	5.6	10	4.3	17	9.6	17	11.1	23	18.1	17	18.9	84	10.8
Total	198	100.0	582	100.0	421	100.0	359	100.0	232	100.0	178	100.0	153	100.0	127	100.0	90	100.0	780	100.0

Table continues p. 92

Table continued from p. 91

	Institution type				Institution control				Number of entering first-year students											
	Two-year		Four-year		Public		Private		Less than 500		501-1,000		1,001-2,000		2,001-4,000		More than 4,000		Total	
Survey question/responses	Freq.	%	Freq.	%	Freq.	%	Freq.	%	Freq.	%	Freq.	%	Freq.	%	Freq.	%	Freq.	%	Freq.	%
Q28. Who teaches the first-year seminar?																				
Adjunct faculty	145	73.2	259	44.5	259	61.7	145	40.4	87	37.5	95	53.4	87	56.9	78	61.9	57	63.3	404	51.9
Full-time non-tenure-track faculty	107	54.0	366	62.9	246	58.6	227	63.2	130	56.0	106	59.6	98	64.1	80	63.5	59	65.6	473	60.7
Tenure-track faculty	104	52.5	450	77.3	281	66.9	273	76.0	157	67.7	131	73.6	117	76.5	85	67.5	64	71.1	554	71.1
Student affairs professionals	111	56.1	294	50.5	241	57.4	164	45.7	118	50.9	87	48.9	73	47.7	73	57.9	54	60.0	405	52.0
Other campus professionals (please specify)	39	19.7	209	35.9	129	30.7	119	33.1	74	31.9	54	30.3	37	24.2	51	40.5	32	35.6	248	31.8
Graduate students	0	0.0	37	6.4	31	7.4	6	1.7	2	0.9	1	0.6	6	3.9	15	11.9	13	14.4	37	4.7
Undergraduate students	0	0.0	32	5.5	16	3.8	16	4.5	8	3.4	5	2.8	6	3.9	6	4.8	7	7.8	32	4.1
Total	198	100.0	582	100.0	420	100.0	359	100.0	232	100.0	178	100.0	153	100.0	126	100.0	90	100.0	779	100.0
Q29. Faculty who teach the first-year seminar teach the course as which of the following?																				
Part of regular teaching load	157	84.0	362	71.5	275	73.7	244	76.3	155	76.0	127	79.4	104	73.8	76	69.1	57	73.1	519	74.9
An additional course beyond regular teaching load	98	52.4	232	45.8	193	51.7	137	42.8	94	46.1	70	43.8	64	45.4	57	51.8	45	57.7	330	47.6
Other (please specify)	11	5.9	25	4.9	24	6.4	48	15.0	10	4.9	5	3.1	8	5.7	8	7.3	5	6.4	36	5.2
Total	187	100.0	506	100.0	373	100.0	320	100.0	204	100.0	160	100.0	141	100.0	110	100.0	78	100.0	693	100.0
Q30. Staff (student affairs and other campus professionals) who teach the first-year seminar teach the course as which of the following?																				
An assigned responsibility	50	40.3	135	40.1	110	42.6	75	36.9	57	39.6	45	43.7	30	37.5	38	45.8	15	29.4	185	40.1
An extra responsibility	84	67.7	249	73.9	180	69.8	153	75.4	104	72.2	73	70.9	57	71.3	59	71.1	40	78.4	333	72.2
Other (please specify)	22	17.7	41	12.2	43	16.7	20	9.9	10	6.9	13	12.6	9	11.3	18	21.7	13	25.5	63	13.7
Total	124	100.0	337	100.0	258	100.0	203	100.0	144	100.0	103	100.0	80	100.0	83	100.0	51	100.0	461	100.0

	Institution type				Institution control				Number of entering first-year students										Total	
	Two-year		Four-year		Public		Private		Less than 500		501-1,000		1,001-2,000		2,001-4,000		More than 4,000			
Survey question/responses	Freq.	%	Freq.	%	Freq.	%	Freq.	%	Freq.	%	Freq.	%	Freq.	%	Freq.	%	Freq.	%	Freq.	%
Q31. Graduate students who teach the first-year seminar teach the course as which of the following?																				
An assigned responsibility	0	-	17	56.7	17	68.0	0	0.0	0	0.0	0	0.0	1	25.0	8	66.7	8	72.7	17	56.7
An extra responsibility	0	-	11	36.7	7	28.0	4	80.0	1	50.0	1	100.0	4	100.0	2	16.7	3	27.3	11	36.7
Other (please specify)	0	-	5	16.7	4	16.0	1	20.0	1	50.0	0	0.0	0	0.0	3	25.0	1	9.1	5	16.7
Total	0	-	30	100.0	25	100.0	5	100.0	2	100.0	1	100.0	4	100.0	12	100.0	11	100.0	30	100.0
Q32. If the first-year seminar is taught as an additional course or as an extra responsibility, what type of compensation is offered for teaching a first year seminar?																				
Direct monetary compensation or stipend	115	91.3	270	83.3	209	83.6	176	88.0	115	83.9	88	91.7	72	83.7	68	89.5	42	76.4	385	85.6
Graduate student support	0	0.0	6	1.9	5	2.0	1	0.5	1	0.7	0	0.0	1	1.2	1	1.3	3	5.5	6	1.3
Professional development funds	1	0.8	15	4.6	11	4.4	5	2.5	3	2.2	3	3.1	2	2.3	5	6.6	3	5.5	16	3.6
Release time	15	11.9	18	5.6	23	9.2	10	5.0	11	8.0	5	5.2	7	8.1	9	11.8	1	1.8	33	7.3
No additional compensation	9	7.1	56	17.3	39	15.6	26	13.0	24	17.5	12	12.5	12	14.0	7	9.2	10	18.2	65	14.4
Other (please specify)	7	5.6	19	5.9	19	7.6	7	3.5	7	5.1	0	0.0	10	11.6	3	3.9	6	10.9	26	5.8
Total	126	100.0	324	100.0	250	100.0	200	100.0	137	100.0	96	100.0	86	100.0	76	100.0	55	100.0	450	100.0
Q37. Is instructor training offered for first-year seminar instructors?																				
Yes	108	71.5	328	69.3	227	68.2	209	71.8	122	71.3	110	72.4	81	62.3	77	72.0	46	71.9	436	69.9
No	41	27.2	140	29.6	103	30.9	78	26.8	48	28.1	42	27.6	46	35.4	29	27.1	16	25.0	181	29.0
I don't know	2	1.3	5	1.1	3	0.9	4	1.4	1	0.6	0	0.0	3	2.3	1	0.9	2	3.1	7	1.1
Total	151	100.0	473	100.0	333	100.0	291	100.0	171	100.0	152	100.0	130	100.0	107	100.0	64	100.0	624	100.0

Table continues p. 94

Table continued from p. 93

	Institution type				Institution control				Number of entering first-year students										Total	
	Two-year		Four-year		Public		Private		Less than 500		501-1,000		1,001-2,000		2,001-4,000		More than 4,000			
Survey question/responses	Freq.	%	Freq.	%	Freq.	%	Freq.	%	Freq.	%	Freq.	%	Freq.	%	Freq.	%	Freq.	%	Freq.	%
Q39. How long is the initial instructor training?																				
Half a day or less	73	48.3	176	37.2	143	42.9	106	36.4	67	39.2	70	46.1	54	41.5	37	34.6	21	32.8	249	39.9
1 day	36	23.8	126	26.6	79	23.7	83	28.5	44	25.7	39	25.7	39	30.0	23	21.5	17	26.6	162	26.0
2 days	11	7.3	69	14.6	40	12.0	40	13.7	22	12.9	19	12.5	14	10.8	16	15.0	9	14.1	80	12.8
3 days	9	6.0	17	3.6	17	5.1	9	3.1	4	2.3	9	5.9	5	3.8	4	3.7	4	6.3	26	4.2
4 days	1	0.7	13	2.7	7	2.1	7	2.4	4	2.3	2	1.3	1	0.8	7	6.5	0	0.0	14	2.2
1 week	2	1.3	22	4.7	9	2.7	15	5.2	8	4.7	5	3.3	7	5.4	3	2.8	1	1.6	24	3.8
2 weeks	1	0.7	4	0.8	2	0.6	3	1.0	2	1.2	0	0.0	2	1.5	0	0.0	1	1.6	5	0.8
Other (please specify)	18	11.9	46	9.7	36	10.8	28	9.6	20	11.7	8	5.3	8	6.2	17	15.9	11	17.2	64	10.3
Total	151	100.0	473	100.0	333	100.0	291	100.0	171	100.0	152	100.0	130	100.0	107	100.0	64	100.0	624	100.0
Q40. Is there ongoing instructor development after initial training?																				
Yes (please explain)	107	70.9	364	77.0	253	76.0	218	74.9	118	69.0	115	75.7	95	73.1	91	85.0	52	81.3	471	75.5
No	44	29.1	109	23.0	80	24.0	73	25.1	53	31.0	37	24.3	35	26.9	16	15.0	12	18.8	153	24.5
Total	151	100.0	473	100.0	333	100.0	291	100.0	171	100.0	152	100.0	130	100.0	107	100.0	64	100.0	624	100.0
Q41. If undergraduate students assist in the first-year seminar, what is their primary role?																				
They teach independently	1	0.5	16	2.8	13	3.2	4	1.1	2	0.9	3	1.7	3	2.0	7	5.7	2	2.3	17	2.2
They teach as a part of a team	5	2.6	90	15.7	46	11.2	49	13.9	35	15.4	18	10.3	8	5.3	20	16.3	14	16.3	95	12.4
They assist the instructor, but do not teach	12	6.3	195	34.0	83	20.1	124	35.2	65	28.5	56	32.0	39	25.7	31	25.2	16	18.6	207	27.1
Other (please specify)	8	4.2	106	18.5	52	12.6	62	17.6	36	15.8	28	16.0	22	14.5	18	14.6	10	11.6	114	14.9
Undergraduate students do not assist in the seminar	168	88.4	242	42.2	261	63.3	149	42.3	115	50.4	87	49.7	91	59.9	65	52.8	52	60.5	410	53.7
Total	190	100.0	574	100.0	412	100.0	352	100.0	228	100.0	175	100.0	152	100.0	123	100.0	86	100.0	764	100.0

	Institution type				Institution control				Number of entering first-year students											
	Two-year		Four-year		Public		Private		Less than 500		501-1,000		1,001-2,000		2,001-4,000		More than 4,000		Total	
Survey question/responses	**Freq.**	**%**	**Freq.**	**%**	**Freq.**	**%**	**Freq.**	**%**	**Freq.**	**%**	**Freq.**	**%**	**Freq.**	**%**	**Freq.**	**%**	**Freq.**	**%**	**Freq.**	**%**
Q42. Please indicate the approximate percentage of sections that are team taught:																				
No sections are team taught	125	65.8	274	47.7	213	51.7	186	52.8	118	51.8	94	53.7	84	55.3	66	53.7	37	43.0	399	52.2
Less than 10%	43	22.6	143	24.9	113	27.4	73	20.7	40	17.5	48	27.4	41	27.0	30	24.4	27	31.4	186	24.3
10-19%	7	3.7	31	5.4	20	4.9	18	5.1	11	4.8	10	5.7	6	3.9	6	4.9	5	5.8	38	5.0
20-29%	2	1.1	13	2.3	8	1.9	7	2.0	7	3.1	4	2.3	0	0.0	3	2.4	1	1.2	15	2.0
30-39%	0	0.0	12	2.1	7	1.7	5	1.4	5	2.2	0	0.0	3	2.0	2	1.6	2	2.3	12	1.6
40-49%	0	0.0	2	0.3	1	0.2	1	0.3	1	0.4	0	0.0	0	0.0	1	0.8	0	0.0	2	0.3
50-59%	2	1.1	7	1.2	6	1.5	3	0.9	2	0.9	2	1.1	1	0.7	1	0.8	3	3.5	9	1.2
60-69%	0	0.0	2	0.3	1	0.2	1	0.3	0	0.0	0	0.0	1	0.7	0	0.0	1	1.2	2	0.3
70-79%	0	0.0	5	0.9	3	0.7	2	0.6	2	0.9	0	0.0	3	2.0	0	0.0	0	0.0	5	0.7
80-89%	0	0.0	5	0.9	2	0.5	3	0.9	3	1.3	0	0.0	0	0.0	2	1.6	0	0.0	5	0.7
90-99%	1	0.5	11	1.9	6	1.5	6	1.7	7	3.1	1	0.6	1	0.7	1	0.8	2	2.3	12	1.6
100%	10	5.3	69	12.0	32	7.8	47	13.4	32	14.0	16	9.1	12	7.9	11	8.9	8	9.3	79	10.3
Total	190	100.0	574	100.0	412	100.0	352	100.0	228	100.0	175	100.0	152	100.0	123	100.0	86	100.0	764	100.0
Q44. What is the approximate percentage of students placed in sections with their academic advisors?																				
No students are placed in sections with their academic advisors	84	44.2	211	36.8	177	43.1	118	33.5	77	33.8	67	38.3	59	39.1	49	39.0	43	50.0	295	30.7
Less than 10%	37	19.5	83	14.5	80	19.5	40	11.4	28	12.3	25	14.3	29	19.2	23	18.7	15	17.4	120	15.7
10-19%	14	7.4	25	4.4	28	6.8	11	3.1	12	5.3	7	4.0	7	4.6	9	7.3	4	4.7	39	5.1
20-29%	4	2.1	28	4.9	26	6.3	6	1.7	5	2.2	6	3.4	9	6.0	7	5.7	5	5.8	32	4.2
30-39%	3	1.6	16	2.8	11	2.7	8	2.3	8	3.5	2	1.1	3	2.0	3	2.4	3	3.5	19	2.5
40-49%	1	0.5	3	0.5	2	0.5	2	0.6	3	1.3	0	0.0	0	0.0	1	0.8	0	0.0	4	0.5

Table continues p. 96

Table continued from p. 95

	Institution type				Institution control				Number of entering first-year students										Total	
	Two-year		Four-year		Public		Private		Less than 500		501-1,000		1,001-2,000		2,001-4,000		More than 4,000			
Survey question/responses	Freq.	%	Freq.	%	Freq.	%	Freq.	%	Freq.	%	Freq.	%	Freq.	%	Freq.	%	Freq.	%	Freq.	%
Q44. What is the approximate percentage of students placed in sections with their academic advisors? *(cont.)*																				
50-59%	0	0.0	16	2.8	4	1.0	12	3.4	8	3.5	2	1.1	2	1.3	4	3.3	0	0.0	16	2.1
60-69%	3	1.6	4	0.7	4	1.0	3	0.9	1	0.4	2	1.1	2	1.3	1	0.8	1	1.2	7	0.9
70-79%	3	1.6	5	0.9	4	1.0	4	1.1	2	0.9	3	1.7	1	0.7	2	1.6	0	0.0	8	1.0
80-89%	4	2.1	9	1.6	5	1.2	8	2.3	3	1.3	3	1.7	1	0.7	5	4.1	1	1.2	13	1.7
90-99%	3	1.6	22	3.8	11	2.7	14	4.0	10	4.4	4	2.3	6	4.0	4	3.3	1	1.2	25	3.3
100%	8	4.2	94	16.4	19	4.6	83	23.6	47	20.6	32	18.3	16	10.6	4	3.3	3	3.5	102	13.4
I don't know	26	13.7	57	9.9	40	9.7	43	12.2	24	10.5	22	12.6	16	10.6	11	8.9	10	11.6	83	10.9
Total	190	100.0	573	100.0	411	100.0	352	100.0	228	100.0	175	100.0	151	100.0	123	100.0	86	100.0	763	100.0
Q45. What is the typical duration of a section of the first-year seminar?																				
Half a term	33	17.4	44	7.7	47	11.4	30	8.5	27	11.8	20	11.4	12	7.9	13	10.6	5	5.8	77	10.1
One quarter	4	2.1	17	3.0	11	2.7	10	2.8	4	1.8	5	2.9	8	5.3	3	2.4	1	1.2	21	2.8
One semester	138	72.6	418	72.9	310	75.4	246	69.9	161	70.6	124	70.9	112	74.2	93	75.6	66	76.7	556	72.9
One year	1	0.5	41	7.2	10	2.4	32	9.1	17	7.5	12	6.9	8	5.3	3	2.4	2	2.3	42	5.5
Other (please specify)	14	7.4	53	9.2	33	8.0	34	9.7	19	8.3	14	8.0	11	7.3	11	8.9	12	14.0	67	8.8
Total	190	100.0	573	100.0	411	100.0	352	100.0	228	100.0	175	100.0	151	100.0	123	100.0	86	100.0	763	100.0
Q46. How many total classroom contact hours are there per week in the first-year seminar?																				
1 hour	48	25.3	181	31.6	117	28.5	112	31.8	72	31.6	49	28.0	43	28.5	35	28.5	30	34.9	229	30.0
2 hours	47	24.7	123	21.5	112	27.3	58	16.5	51	22.4	41	23.4	28	18.5	34	27.6	16	18.6	170	22.3
3 hours	84	44.2	209	36.5	160	38.9	133	37.8	82	36.0	66	37.7	62	41.1	49	39.8	34	39.5	293	38.4
4 hours	4	2.1	47	8.2	14	3.4	37	10.5	15	6.6	17	9.7	17	11.3	1	0.8	1	1.2	51	6.7
5 hours	1	0.5	3	0.5	1	0.2	3	0.9	1	0.4	2	1.1	0	0.0	0	0.0	1	1.2	4	0.5
6 or more hours	6	3.2	10	1.7	7	1.7	9	2.6	7	3.1	0	0.0	1	0.7	4	3.3	4	4.7	16	2.1
Total	190	100.0	573	100.0	411	100.0	352	100.0	228	100.0	175	100.0	151	100.0	123	100.0	86	100.0	763	100.0

	Institution type				Institution control				Number of entering first-year students										Total	
	Two-year		Four-year		Public		Private		Less than 500		501-1,000		1,001-2,000		2,001-4,000		More than 4,000			
Survey question/responses	Freq.	%	Freq.	%	Freq.	%	Freq.	%	Freq.	%	Freq.	%	Freq.	%	Freq.	%	Freq.	%	Freq.	%
Q47. Does the first-year seminar carry academic credit?																				
Yes	177	93.2	544	94.9	387	94.2	334	94.9	213	93.4	166	94.9	142	94.0	119	96.7	81	94.2	721	94.5
No	13	6.8	29	5.1	24	5.8	18	5.1	15	6.6	9	5.1	9	6.0	4	3.3	5	5.8	42	5.5
Total	190	100.0	573	100.0	411	100.0	352	100.0	228	100.0	175	100.0	151	100.0	123	100.0	86	100.0	763	100.0
Q48. How many credits does the first-year seminar carry?																				
1 credit	82	46.6	231	42.5	176	45.6	137	41.0	95	44.6	74	44.6	51	35.9	57	48.3	36	44.4	313	43.5
2 credits	19	10.8	65	11.9	58	15.0	26	7.8	23	10.8	16	9.6	19	13.4	15	12.7	11	13.6	84	11.7
3 credits	72	40.9	156	28.7	138	35.8	90	26.9	62	29.1	42	25.3	50	35.2	42	35.6	32	39.5	228	31.7
4 credits	1	0.6	75	13.8	10	2.6	66	19.8	23	10.8	29	17.5	20	14.1	3	2.5	1	1.2	76	10.6
5 credits	1	0.6	2	0.4	1	0.3	2	0.6	2	0.9	1	0.6	0	0.0	0	0.0	0	0.0	3	0.4
6 or more credits	1	0.6	15	2.8	3	0.8	13	3.9	8	3.8	4	2.4	2	1.4	1	0.8	1	1.2	16	2.2
Total	176	100.0	544	100.0	386	100.0	334	100.0	213	100.0	166	100.0	142	100.0	118	100.0	81	100.0	720	100.0
Q49. How is the first-year seminar credit applied?																				
As an elective	104	59.1	169	31.1	216	56.0	57	17.1	46	21.6	56	33.7	57	40.1	59	50.0	55	67.9	273	37.9
Toward general education requirements	68	38.6	354	65.1	157	40.7	265	79.3	158	74.2	107	64.5	77	54.2	55	46.6	25	30.9	422	58.6
Toward major requirements	20	11.4	41	7.5	39	10.1	22	6.6	11	5.2	18	10.8	17	12.0	9	7.6	6	7.4	61	8.5
Other (please specify)	15	8.5	65	11.9	43	11.1	37	11.1	18	8.5	20	12.0	19	13.4	13	11.0	10	12.3	80	11.1
Total	176	100.0	544	100.0	386	100.0	334	100.0	213	100.0	166	100.0	142	100.0	118	100.0	81	100.0	720	100.0
Q50. How is the first-year seminar graded?																				
Letter grade	166	87.8	483	84.3	359	87.6	290	82.4	178	78.1	151	86.3	129	85.4	112	91.8	79	91.9	649	85.2
Pass/fail	21	11.1	70	12.2	41	10.0	50	14.2	42	18.4	22	12.6	16	10.6	10	8.2	1	1.2	91	11.9
No grade	1	0.5	8	1.4	4	1.0	5	1.4	2	0.9	2	1.1	3	2.0	0	0.0	2	2.3	9	1.2
Other (please specify)	1	0.5	12	2.1	6	1.5	7	2.0	6	2.6	0	0.0	3	2.0	0	0.0	4	4.7	13	1.7
Total	189	100.0	573	100.0	410	100.0	352	100.0	228	100.0	175	100.0	151	100.0	122	100.0	86	100.0	762	100.0

Table continues p. 98

Table continued from p. 97

	Institution type				Institution control				Number of entering first-year students										Total	
	Two-year		Four-year		Public		Private		Less than 500		501-1,000		1,001-2,000		2,001-4,000		More than 4,000			
Survey question/responses	**Freq.**	**%**	**Freq.**	**%**	**Freq.**	**%**	**Freq.**	**%**	**Freq.**	**%**	**Freq.**	**%**	**Freq.**	**%**	**Freq.**	**%**	**Freq.**	**%**	**Freq.**	**%**
Q51. Do any sections incorporate online components?																				
I don't know	9	4.8	54	9.4	29	7.1	34	9.7	18	7.9	12	6.9	12	7.9	9	7.4	12	14.0	63	8.3
Yes	151	79.9	304	53.1	294	71.7	161	45.7	113	49.6	105	60.0	97	64.2	88	72.1	52	60.5	455	59.7
No	29	15.3	215	37.5	87	21.2	157	44.6	97	42.5	58	33.1	42	27.8	25	20.5	22	25.6	244	32.0
Total	189	100.0	573	100.0	410	100.0	352	100.0	228	100.0	175	100.0	151	100.0	122	100.0	86	100.0	762	100.0
Q53. Are there any online-only sections?																				
I don't know	9	4.8	54	9.4	29	7.1	34	9.7	18	7.9	12	6.9	12	7.9	9	7.4	12	14.0	63	8.3
Yes	151	79.9	304	53.1	294	71.7	161	45.7	113	49.6	105	60.0	97	64.2	88	72.1	52	60.5	455	59.7
No	29	15.3	215	37.5	87	21.2	157	44.6	97	42.5	58	33.1	42	27.8	25	20.5	22	25.6	244	32.0
Total	189	100.0	573	100.0	410	100.0	352	100.0	228	100.0	175	100.0	151	100.0	122	100.0	86	100.0	762	100.0
Q54. Please indicate the approximate percentage of online-only sections:																				
Less than 10%	37	41.6	39	79.6	68	56.7	8	44.4	7	38.9	15	62.5	20	50.0	19	57.6	15	65.2	76	55.1
10-19%	20	22.5	4	8.2	20	16.7	4	22.2	5	27.8	3	12.5	8	20.0	6	18.2	2	8.7	24	17.4
20-29%	14	15.7	3	6.1	15	12.5	2	11.1	3	16.7	4	16.7	4	10.0	5	15.2	1	4.3	17	12.3
30-39%	7	7.9	1	2.0	7	5.8	1	5.6	2	11.1	0	0.0	2	5.0	2	6.1	2	8.7	8	5.8
40-49%	4	4.5	0	0.0	4	3.3	0	0.0	0	0.0	0	0.0	3	7.5	0	0.0	1	4.3	4	2.9
50-59%	2	2.2	0	0.0	1	0.8	1	5.6	0	0.0	1	4.2	0	0.0	1	3.0	0	0.0	2	1.4
60-69%	1	1.1	0	0.0	1	0.8	0	0.0	0	0.0	1	4.2	0	0.0	0	0.0	0	0.0	1	0.7
70 - 79%	0	0.0	0	0.0	0	0.0	0	0.0	0	0.0	0	0.0	0	0.0	0	0.0	0	0.0	0	0.0
80-89%	0	0.0	1	2.0	0	0.0	1	5.6	0	0.0	0	0.0	0	0.0	0	0.0	1	4.3	1	0.7
90-99%	1	1.1	0	0.0	1	0.8	0	0.0	1	5.6	0	0.0	0	0.0	0	0.0	0	0.0	1	0.7
100%	3	3.4	1	2.0	3	2.5	1	5.6	0	0.0	0	0.0	3	7.5	0	0.0	1	4.3	4	2.9
Total	89	100.0	49	100.0	120	100.0	18	100.0	18	100.0	24	100.0	40	100.0	33	100.0	23	100.0	138	100.0

	Institution type				Institution control				Number of entering first-year students										Total	
	Two-year		Four-year		Public		Private		Less than 500		501-1,000		1,001-2,000		2,001-4,000		More than 4,000			
Survey question/responses	Freq.	%	Freq.	%	Freq.	%	Freq.	%	Freq.	%	Freq.	%	Freq.	%	Freq.	%	Freq.	%	Freq.	%
Q55. Select the three most important course objectives for the first-year seminar:																				
Create common first-year experience	30	16.0	134	23.4	67	16.4	97	27.6	73	32.0	34	19.5	28	18.5	17	13.9	12	14.0	164	21.6
Develop a connection with the institution	84	44.7	258	45.0	199	48.7	143	40.6	99	43.4	77	44.3	70	46.4	61	50.0	35	40.7	342	44.9
Develop academic skills	71	37.8	205	35.8	168	41.1	108	30.7	69	30.3	65	37.4	63	41.7	47	38.5	32	37.2	276	36.3
Develop critical-thinking skills	27	14.4	150	26.2	72	17.6	105	29.8	52	22.8	41	23.6	36	23.8	28	23.0	20	23.3	177	23.3
Develop financial literacy	8	4.3	4	0.7	9	2.2	3	0.9	6	2.6	1	0.6	1	0.7	1	0.8	3	3.5	12	1.6
Develop information literacy	11	5.9	45	7.9	24	5.9	32	9.1	17	7.5	14	8.0	13	8.6	7	5.7	5	5.8	56	7.4
Develop oral communication skills	2	1.1	31	5.4	7	1.7	26	7.4	11	4.8	12	6.9	8	5.3	1	0.8	1	1.2	33	4.3
Develop study skills	84	44.7	68	11.9	115	28.1	37	10.5	41	18.0	30	17.2	33	21.9	29	23.8	19	22.1	152	20.0
Develop support network or friendships	23	12.2	87	15.2	56	13.7	54	15.3	36	15.8	26	14.9	17	11.3	18	14.8	13	15.1	110	14.5
Develop writing skills	1	0.5	87	15.2	11	2.7	77	21.9	38	16.7	30	17.2	12	7.9	8	6.6	0	0.0	88	11.6
Develop intercultural competence	2	1.1	4	0.7	4	1.0	2	0.6	2	0.9	1	0.6	2	1.3	0	0.0	1	1.2	6	0.8
Improve second-year return rates	26	13.8	84	14.7	62	15.2	48	13.6	44	19.3	25	14.4	10	6.6	21	17.2	10	11.6	110	14.5
Increase student-faculty interaction	11	5.9	83	14.5	51	12.5	43	12.2	18	7.9	17	9.8	28	18.5	15	12.3	16	18.6	94	12.4
Introduce a discipline	3	1.6	35	6.1	24	5.9	14	4.0	3	1.3	8	4.6	8	5.3	9	7.4	10	11.6	38	5.0
Introduce the liberal arts	1	0.5	62	10.8	14	3.4	49	13.9	27	11.8	21	12.1	7	4.6	4	3.3	4	4.7	63	8.3
Provide orientation to campus resources and services	90	47.9	198	34.6	187	45.7	101	28.7	77	33.8	61	35.1	60	39.7	52	42.6	38	44.2	288	37.8
Provide career exploration	24	12.8	24	4.2	37	9.0	11	3.1	9	3.9	11	6.3	8	5.3	11	9.0	9	10.5	48	6.3
Provide preprofessional preparation	1	0.5	14	2.4	10	2.4	5	1.4	3	1.3	1	0.6	3	2.0	2	1.6	6	7.0	15	2.0
Self-exploration or personal development	50	26.6	79	13.8	73	17.8	56	15.9	38	16.7	25	14.4	27	17.9	21	17.2	18	20.9	129	17.0
Other (please specify)	13	6.9	49	8.6	28	6.8	34	9.7	16	7.0	15	8.6	14	9.3	12	9.8	5	5.8	62	8.1
Total	188	100.0	573	100.0	409	100.0	352	100.0	228	100.0	174	100.0	151	100.0	122	100.0	86	100.0	761	100.0

Table continues p. 100

Table continued from p 99

	Institution type				Institution control				Number of entering first-year students											
	Two-year		Four-year		Public		Private		Less than 500		501-1,000		1,001-2,000		2,001-4,000		More than 4,000		Total	
Survey question/responses	Freq.	%	Freq.	%	Freq.	%	Freq.	%	Freq.	%	Freq.	%	Freq.	%	Freq.	%	Freq.	%	Freq.	%
Q56. Select the three most important topics that compose the content of this first-year seminar:																				
Academic planning or advising	84	44.7	180	31.4	164	40.1	100	28.4	71	31.1	61	35.1	51	33.8	54	44.3	27	31.4	264	34.7
Career exploration or preparation	55	29.3	75	13.1	95	23.2	35	9.9	29	12.7	22	12.6	25	16.6	32	26.2	22	25.6	130	17.1
Campus engagement	42	22.3	169	29.5	104	25.4	107	30.4	65	28.5	56	32.2	37	24.5	33	27.0	20	23.3	211	27.7
Campus resources	90	47.9	182	31.8	186	45.5	86	24.4	69	30.3	58	33.3	64	42.4	45	36.9	36	41.9	272	35.7
College policies and procedures	31	16.5	63	11.0	62	15.2	32	9.1	29	12.7	15	8.6	24	15.9	17	13.9	9	10.5	94	12.4
Critical thinking	33	17.6	215	37.5	91	22.2	157	44.6	82	36.0	64	36.8	54	35.8	29	23.8	19	22.1	248	32.6
Diversity issues	7	3.7	29	5.1	20	4.9	16	4.5	9	3.9	6	3.4	8	5.3	5	4.1	8	9.3	36	4.7
Financial literacy	10	5.3	8	1.4	13	3.2	5	1.4	6	2.6	5	2.9	3	2.0	1	0.8	3	3.5	18	2.4
Global learning	0	0.0	25	4.4	11	2.7	14	4.0	6	2.6	4	2.3	5	3.3	6	4.9	4	4.7	25	3.3
Health and wellness	1	0.5	10	1.7	5	1.2	6	1.7	5	2.2	5	2.9	0	0.0	0	0.0	1	1.2	11	1.4
Information literacy	11	5.9	66	11.5	31	7.6	46	13.1	29	12.7	18	10.3	14	9.3	9	7.4	7	8.1	77	10.1
Oral communication skills	1	0.5	38	6.6	11	2.7	28	8.0	16	7.0	11	6.3	8	5.3	1	0.8	3	3.5	39	5.1
Relationship issues (e.g., interpersonal skills, conflict resolution)	16	8.5	42	7.3	21	5.1	37	10.5	26	11.4	15	8.6	5	3.3	6	4.9	6	7.0	58	7.6
Specific disciplinary topic	5	2.7	95	16.6	42	10.3	58	16.5	22	9.6	26	14.9	22	14.6	14	11.5	16	18.6	100	13.1
Study skills	95	50.5	132	23.0	173	42.3	54	15.3	52	22.8	43	24.7	52	34.4	49	40.2	31	36.0	227	29.8
Time management	63	33.5	109	19.0	113	27.6	59	16.8	51	22.4	33	19.0	33	21.9	32	26.2	23	26.7	172	22.6
Writing skills	4	2.1	128	22.3	30	7.3	102	29.0	53	23.2	37	21.3	23	15.2	14	11.5	5	5.8	132	17.3
Other (please specify)	13	6.9	93	16.2	38	9.3	68	19.3	42	18.4	24	13.8	14	9.3	17	13.9	9	10.5	106	13.9
Total	188	100.0	573	100.0	409	100.0	352	100.0	228	100.0	174	100.0	151	100.0	122	100.0	86	100.0	761	100.0

	Institution type				Institution control				Number of entering first-year students										Total	
	Two-year		Four-year		Public		Private		Less than 500		501-1,000		1,001-2,000		2,001-4,000		More than 4,000			
Survey question/responses	**Freq.**	**%**	**Freq.**	**%**	**Freq.**	**%**	**Freq.**	**%**	**Freq.**	**%**	**Freq.**	**%**	**Freq.**	**%**	**Freq.**	**%**	**Freq.**	**%**	**Freq.**	**%**
Q57. Which of the following approaches associated with high-impact educational practices are intentionally incorporated into the first-year seminar? (Select all that apply):																				
Writing-intensive experiences	56	29.8	267	46.7	145	35.5	178	50.6	98	43.0	80	46.0	63	41.7	52	43.0	30	34.9	323	42.5
Collaboration and teamwork	132	70.2	379	66.3	299	73.3	212	60.2	142	62.3	114	65.5	107	70.9	87	71.9	61	70.9	511	67.2
Diversity and global learning	88	46.8	359	62.8	240	58.8	207	58.8	117	51.3	103	59.2	93	61.6	75	62.0	59	68.6	447	58.8
None of the above	35	18.6	61	10.7	52	12.7	44	12.5	40	17.5	13	7.5	17	11.3	14	11.6	12	14.0	96	12.6
Total	188	100.0	572	100.0	408	100.0	352	100.0	228	100.0	174	100.0	151	100.0	121	100.0	86	100.0	760	100.0
Q59. Which of the following high-impact educational practices are connected to the first-year seminar? (Select all that apply):																				
Service-learning	30	16.1	209	37.0	106	26.2	133	38.4	82	36.6	52	30.4	38	25.2	42	35.0	25	29.4	239	31.8
Learning community	61	32.8	215	38.1	172	42.5	104	30.1	62	27.7	60	35.1	58	38.4	52	43.3	44	51.8	276	36.8
Common reading experience	27	14.5	259	45.8	120	29.6	166	48.0	92	41.1	70	40.9	48	31.8	45	37.5	31	36.5	286	38.1
Undergraduate research	8	4.3	88	15.6	45	11.1	51	14.7	24	10.7	24	14.0	20	13.2	11	9.2	17	20.0	96	12.8
None of the above	97	52.2	136	24.1	151	37.3	82	23.7	65	29.0	52	30.4	51	33.8	40	33.3	25	29.4	233	31.0
Total	186	100.0	565	100.0	405	100.0	346	100.0	224	100.0	171	100.0	151	100.0	120	100.0	85	100.0	751	100.0
Q60. How many total hours are students required to complete for the service-learning component?																				
There is no requirement about the total number of hours.	14	46.7	87	41.8	52	49.5	49	36.8	25	30.5	24	46.2	17	44.7	23	56.1	12	48.0	101	42.4
5 or fewer	10	33.3	64	30.8	32	30.5	42	31.6	31	37.8	18	34.6	11	28.9	8	19.5	6	24.0	74	31.1
6-10	3	10.0	45	21.6	15	14.3	33	24.8	20	24.4	9	17.3	7	18.4	7	17.1	5	20.0	48	20.2
11-15	0	0.0	3	1.4	1	1.0	2	1.5	2	2.4	0	0.0	1	2.6	0	0.0	0	0.0	3	1.3
16-20	1	3.3	6	2.9	2	1.9	5	3.8	2	2.4	1	1.9	2	5.3	0	0.0	2	8.0	7	2.9
More than 20	2	6.7	3	1.4	3	2.9	2	1.5	2	2.4	0	0.0	0	0.0	3	7.3	0	0.0	5	2.1
Total	30	100.0	208	100.0	105	100.0	133	100.0	82	100.0	52	100.0	38	100.0	41	100.0	25	100.0	238	100.0

Table continues p. 102

Table continued from p. 101

	Institution type				Institution control				Number of entering first-year students										Total	
	Two-year		Four-year		Public		Private		Less than 500		501-1,000		1,001-2,000		2,001-4,000		More than 4,000			
Survey question/responses	**Freq.**	**%**	**Freq.**	**%**	**Freq.**	**%**	**Freq.**	**%**	**Freq.**	**%**	**Freq.**	**%**	**Freq.**	**%**	**Freq.**	**%**	**Freq.**	**%**	**Freq.**	**%**
Q61. Which of the following are used as reflection techniques in the first-year seminar associated with the service-learning component? (Select all that apply):																				
Class discussion	24	80.0	160	76.9	83	79.0	101	75.9	59	72.0	38	73.1	33	86.8	33	80.5	21	84.0	184	77.3
Portfolio	6	20.0	42	20.2	21	20.0	27	20.3	16	19.5	5	9.6	12	31.6	11	26.8	4	16.0	48	20.2
Student presentations	18	60.0	101	48.6	63	60.0	56	42.1	25	30.5	26	50.0	25	65.8	27	65.9	16	64.0	119	50.0
Writing exercise, such as writing a paper or journaling	22	73.3	162	77.9	80	76.2	104	78.2	61	74.4	38	73.1	36	94.7	29	70.7	20	80.0	184	77.3
Other (please specify)	3	10.0	20	9.6	12	11.4	11	8.3	5	6.1	5	9.6	3	7.9	3	7.3	7	28.0	23	9.7
There is no reflection associated with the service-learning component.	1	3.3	10	4.8	2	1.9	9	6.8	7	8.5	1	1.9	1	2.6	2	4.9	0	0.0	11	4.6
Total	30	100.0	208	100.0	105	100.0	133	100.0	82	100.0	52	100.0	38	100.0	41	100.0	25	100.0	238	100.0
Q63. Which of the following are characteristics of the learning community of which the first-year seminar is a part? (Select all that apply):																				
Co-enrollment, not all courses	45	73.8	158	73.8	135	78.9	68	65.4	36	58.1	43	71.7	46	79.3	40	78.4	38	86.4	203	73.8
Co-enrollment, all other courses	10	16.4	15	7.0	19	11.1	6	5.8	5	8.1	6	10.0	3	5.2	7	13.7	4	9.1	25	9.1
Coordinated course content	24	39.3	71	33.2	63	36.8	32	30.8	21	33.9	27	45.0	15	25.9	19	37.3	13	29.5	95	34.5
Course content connected by common intellectual theme	21	34.4	50	23.4	47	27.5	24	23.1	16	25.8	15	25.0	14	24.1	15	29.4	11	25.0	71	25.8
Common set of theme-based experiences outside of the course	16	26.2	76	35.5	53	31.0	39	37.5	23	37.1	23	38.3	20	34.5	12	23.5	14	31.8	92	33.5
Living-learning community	2	3.3	82	38.3	50	29.2	34	32.7	13	21.0	17	28.3	20	34.5	16	31.4	18	40.9	84	30.5
Other (please specify)	1	1.6	21	9.8	11	6.4	11	10.6	4	6.5	5	8.3	6	10.3	4	7.8	3	6.8	22	8.0
Total	61	100.0	214	100.0	171	100.0	104	100.0	62	100.0	60	100.0	58	100.0	51	100.0	44	100.0	275	100.0

	Institution type				Institution control				Number of entering first-year students										Total	
	Two-year		Four-year		Public		Private		Less than 500		501-1,000		1,001-2,000		2,001-4,000		More than 4,000			
Survey question/responses	Freq.	%	Freq.	%	Freq.	%	Freq.	%	Freq.	%	Freq.	%	Freq.	%	Freq.	%	Freq.	%	Freq.	%
Q67. What campus unit directly administers the first-year seminar?																				
Academic affairs central office	38	20.4	156	27.7	85	21.0	109	31.6	67	29.9	47	27.5	39	25.8	24	20.3	17	20.0	194	25.9
College or school (e.g., College of Liberal Arts)	13	7.0	57	10.1	41	10.1	29	8.4	14	6.3	19	11.1	14	9.3	11	9.3	12	14.1	70	9.3
Academic department(s) (please specify)	70	37.6	80	14.2	102	25.2	48	13.9	48	21.4	20	11.7	35	23.2	28	23.7	19	22.4	150	20.0
First-year program office	13	7.0	109	19.4	69	17.1	53	15.4	24	10.7	35	20.5	23	15.2	22	18.6	18	21.2	122	16.3
Student affairs central office	23	12.4	34	6.0	28	6.9	29	8.4	24	10.7	16	9.4	12	7.9	3	2.5	2	2.4	57	7.6
Other (please specify)	29	15.6	127	22.6	79	19.6	77	22.3	47	21.0	34	19.9	28	18.5	30	25.4	17	20.0	156	20.8
Total	186	100.0	563	100.0	404	100.0	345	100.0	224	100.0	171	100.0	151	100.0	118	100.0	85	100.0	749	100.0
Q68. Which of the following best describes the institutional division where the first-year program office is housed?																				
Academic affairs	4	30.8	72	66.1	35	50.7	41	77.4	18	75.0	23	65.7	14	60.9	10	45.5	11	61.1	76	62.3
Student affairs	7	53.8	19	17.4	20	29.0	6	11.3	2	8.3	10	28.6	5	21.7	6	27.3	3	16.7	26	21.3
Enrollment management	0	0.0	8	7.3	7	10.1	1	1.9	2	8.3	1	2.9	1	4.3	3	13.6	1	5.6	8	6.6
Other (please specify)	2	15.4	10	9.2	7	10.1	5	9.4	2	8.3	1	2.9	3	13.0	3	13.6	3	16.7	12	9.8
Total	13	100.0	109	100.0	69	100.0	53	100.0	24	100.0	35	100.0	23	100.0	22	100.0	18	100.0	122	100.0
Q69. Is there a dean, director, or coordinator of the first-year seminar?																				
Yes	127	68.3	474	84.2	305	75.5	296	85.8	183	81.7	138	80.7	115	76.2	95	80.5	70	82.4	601	80.2
No	57	30.6	86	15.3	94	23.3	49	14.2	41	18.3	32	18.7	35	23.2	21	17.8	14	16.5	143	19.1
I don't know	2	1.1	3	0.5	5	1.2	0	0.0	0	0.0	1	0.6	1	0.7	2	1.7	1	1.2	5	0.7
Total	186	100.0	563	100.0	404	100.0	345	100.0	224	100.0	171	100.0	151	100.0	118	100.0	85	100.0	749	100.0
Q70. Does the dean, director, or coordinator of the first-year seminar work full time or less than full time in this position?																				
Full time (approximately 40 hours a week)	60	47.2	203	42.8	164	53.8	99	33.4	52	28.4	62	44.9	49	42.6	58	61.1	42	60.0	263	43.8
Less than full time	67	52.8	271	57.2	141	46.2	197	66.6	131	71.6	76	55.1	66	57.4	37	38.9	28	40.0	338	56.2
Total	127	100.0	474	100.0	305	100.0	296	100.0	183	100.0	138	100.0	115	100.0	95	100.0	70	100.0	601	100.0

Table continues p. 104

Table continued from p. 103

	Institution type				Institution control				Number of entering first-year students										Total	
	Two-year		Four-year		Public		Private		Less than 500		501-1,000		1,001-2,000		2,001-4,000		More than 4,000			
Survey question/responses	Freq.	%	Freq.	%	Freq.	%	Freq.	%	Freq.	%	Freq.	%	Freq.	%	Freq.	%	Freq.	%	Freq.	%
Q71. Does the dean, director, or coordinator have another position on campus?																				
Yes	64	95.5	265	97.8	136	96.5	193	98.0	128	97.7	74	97.4	65	98.5	36	97.3	26	92.9	329	97.3
No	3	4.5	6	2.2	5	3.5	4	2.0	3	2.3	2	2.6	1	1.5	1	2.7	2	7.1	9	2.7
Total	67	100.0	271	100.0	141	100.0	197	100.0	131	100.0	76	100.0	66	100.0	37	100.0	28	100.0	338	100.0
Q72. The dean, director, or coordinator's other campus role is as which of the following? (Select all that apply):																				
Academic affairs administrator	17	26.6	71	26.8	43	31.6	45	23.3	29	22.7	23	31.1	16	24.6	12	33.3	8	30.8	88	26.7
Faculty member	36	56.3	165	62.3	68	50.0	133	68.9	81	63.3	46	62.2	41	63.1	18	50.0	15	57.7	201	61.1
Student affairs administrator	12	18.8	38	14.3	24	17.6	26	13.5	25	19.5	9	12.2	8	12.3	4	11.1	4	15.4	50	15.2
Other (please specify)	5	7.8	40	15.1	20	14.7	25	13.0	13	10.2	11	14.9	9	13.8	6	16.7	6	23.1	45	13.7
Total	64	100.0	265	100.0	136	100.0	193	100.0	128	100.0	74	100.0	65	100.0	36	100.0	26	100.0	329	100.0
Q73. Has your first-year seminar been formally assessed or evaluated since fall 2009?																				
Yes	92	49.5	353	62.7	227	56.2	218	63.2	133	59.4	99	57.9	93	61.6	69	58.5	51	60.0	445	59.4
No	73	39.2	170	30.2	139	34.4	104	30.1	72	32.1	63	36.8	49	32.5	37	31.4	22	25.9	243	32.4
I don't know	21	11.3	40	7.1	38	9.4	23	6.7	19	8.5	9	5.3	9	6.0	12	10.2	12	14.1	61	8.1
Total	186	100.0	563	100.0	404	100.0	345	100.0	224	100.0	171	100.0	151	100.0	118	100.0	85	100.0	749	100.0
Q74. What type of assessment was conducted? (Select all that apply):																				
Analysis of institutional data (e.g., GPA, retention rates, graduation)	65	71.4	251	71.1	176	77.5	140	64.2	81	60.9	66	66.7	72	77.4	56	82.4	41	80.4	316	71.2
Direct assessment of student learning outcomes	46	50.5	189	53.5	120	52.9	115	52.8	64	48.1	51	51.5	57	61.3	36	52.9	27	52.9	235	52.9
Focus groups with instructors	27	29.7	130	36.8	67	29.5	90	41.3	52	39.1	33	33.3	31	33.3	23	33.8	18	35.3	157	35.4
Focus groups with students	22	24.2	114	32.3	67	29.5	69	31.7	38	28.6	35	35.4	24	25.8	21	30.9	18	35.3	136	30.6
Individual interviews with instructors	12	13.2	77	21.8	43	18.9	46	21.1	25	18.8	16	16.2	17	18.3	18	26.5	13	25.5	89	20.0

Survey question/responses	Institution type: Two-year Freq.	Two-year %	Four-year Freq.	Four-year %	Institution control: Public Freq.	Public %	Private Freq.	Private %	Number of entering first-year students: Less than 500 Freq.	Less than 500 %	501-1,000 Freq.	501-1,000 %	1,001-2,000 Freq.	1,001-2,000 %	2,001-4,000 Freq.	2,001-4,000 %	More than 4,000 Freq.	More than 4,000 %	Total Freq.	Total %
Q74. What type of assessment was conducted? (Select all that apply): *(cont.)*																				
Individual interviews with students	9	9.9	46	13.0	30	13.2	25	11.5	16	12.0	13	13.1	7	7.5	12	17.6	7	13.7	55	12.4
Program review	28	30.8	120	34.0	67	29.5	81	37.2	43	32.3	37	37.4	27	29.0	24	35.3	17	33.3	148	33.3
Student course evaluation	74	81.3	312	88.4	194	85.5	192	88.1	116	87.2	87	87.9	76	81.7	60	88.2	47	92.2	386	86.9
Survey instrument	33	36.3	204	57.8	117	51.5	120	55.0	65	48.9	61	61.6	49	52.7	30	44.1	32	62.7	237	53.4
Total	91	100.0	353	100.0	227	100.0	218	100.0	133	100.0	99	100.0	93	100.0	68	100.0	51	100.0	444	100.0
Q75. What type of survey instrument did your institution use to assess or evaluate the first-year seminar? (Select all that apply):																				
A locally developed (i.e., home-grown) survey of instructors	18	54.5	117	57.4	72	61.5	63	52.5	31	47.7	35	57.4	30	61.2	16	53.3	23	71.9	135	57.0
A locally developed survey of students	23	69.7	155	76.0	87	74.4	91	75.8	49	75.4	44	72.1	38	77.6	21	70.0	26	81.3	178	75.1
A national survey (e.g., NSSE, CCSSE, CIRP, EBI)	19	57.6	111	54.4	66	56.4	64	53.3	33	50.8	36	59.0	28	57.1	15	50.0	18	56.3	130	54.9
I don't know	0	0.0	1	0.5	0	0.0	1	0.8	0	0.0	0	0.0	0	0.0	1	3.3	0	0.0	1	0.4
Total	33	100.0	204	100.0	117	100.0	120	100.0	65	100.0	61	100.0	49	100.0	30	100.0	32	100.0	237	100.0
Q76. Please identify the national survey(s) you used: (Select all that apply):																				
Beginning College Survey of Student Engagement (BCSSE)	0	0.0	20	18.2	8	12.3	12	19.0	5	15.6	6	16.7	8	28.6	0	0.0	1	5.9	20	15.6
College Student Experiences Questionnaire (CSEQ)	0	0.0	0	0.0	0	0.0	0	0.0	0	0.0	0	0.0	0	0.0	0	0.0	0	0.0	0	0.0
Collegiate Learning Assessment (CLA)	0	0.0	17	15.5	8	12.3	9	14.3	5	15.6	6	16.7	5	17.9	1	6.7	0	0.0	17	13.3
Community College Survey of Student Engagement (CCSSE)	17	94.4	1	0.9	15	23.1	3	4.8	4	12.5	6	16.7	2	7.1	1	6.7	5	29.4	18	14.1

Table continues p. 106

Table continued from p. 105

	Institution type				Institution control				Number of entering first-year students											
	Two-year		Four-year		Public		Private		Less than 500		501-1,000		1,001-2,000		2,001-4,000		More than 4,000		Total	
Survey question/responses	Freq.	%	Freq.	%	Freq.	%	Freq.	%	Freq.	%	Freq.	%	Freq.	%	Freq.	%	Freq.	%	Freq.	%
Q76. Please identify the national survey(s) you used: (Select all that apply): *(cont.)*																				
Cooperative Institutional Research Program (CIRP) Freshman Survey	0	0.0	35	31.8	12	18.5	23	36.5	7	21.9	9	25.0	9	32.1	6	40.0	4	23.5	35	27.3
Cooperative Institutional Research Program (CIRP) Your First College Year (YFCY) Survey	0	0.0	10	9.1	3	4.6	7	11.1	3	9.4	3	8.3	2	7.1	2	13.3	0	0.0	10	7.8
Faculty Survey of Student Engagement (FSSE)	1	5.6	10	9.1	3	4.6	8	12.7	5	15.6	2	5.6	3	10.7	0	0.0	1	5.9	11	8.6
First-Year Initiative (FYI)	2	11.1	11	10.0	9	13.8	4	6.3	3	9.4	1	2.8	2	7.1	3	20.0	4	23.5	13	10.2
Individual Developmental and Educational Assessment (IDEA)	1	5.6	5	4.5	1	1.5	5	7.9	2	6.3	2	5.6	1	3.6	0	0.0	1	5.9	6	4.7
National Survey of Student Engagement (NSSE)	0	0.0	97	88.2	44	67.7	53	84.1	26	81.3	28	77.8	23	82.1	11	73.3	9	52.9	97	75.8
Student Satisfaction Inventory (SSI)	1	5.6	17	15.5	5	7.7	13	20.6	6	18.8	4	11.1	4	14.3	2	13.3	2	11.8	18	14.1
Survey of Entering Student Engagement (SENSE)	2	11.1	0	0.0	2	3.1	0	0.0	0	0.0	0	0.0	0	0.0	0	0.0	2	11.8	2	1.6
Other (please specify)	0	0.0	21	19.1	11	16.9	10	15.9	5	15.6	6	16.7	7	25.0	2	13.3	1	5.9	21	16.4
Total	18	100.0	110	100.0	65	100.0	63	100.0	32	100.0	36	100.0	28	100.0	15	100.0	17	100.0	128	100.0
Q78. Please indicate each student outcome that was measured: (Select all that apply):																				
Achievement of learning or course outcomes	59	65.6	244	69.7	155	69.2	148	68.5	92	69.7	66	67.3	58	63.0	52	76.5	35	70.0	303	68.9
Civic engagement	4	4.4	50	14.3	27	12.1	27	12.5	16	12.1	10	10.2	14	15.2	7	10.3	7	14.0	54	12.3
Connections with peers	19	21.1	140	40.0	79	35.3	80	37.0	52	39.4	31	31.6	31	33.7	22	32.4	23	46.0	159	36.1
Critical thinking	30	33.3	131	37.4	77	34.4	84	38.9	48	36.4	34	34.7	32	34.8	29	42.6	18	36.0	161	36.6
Grade point average	47	52.2	127	36.3	113	50.4	61	28.2	35	26.5	33	33.7	45	48.9	38	55.9	23	46.0	174	39.5

	Institution type				Institution control				Number of entering first-year students										Total	
	Two-year		Four-year		Public		Private		Less than 500		501-1,000		1,001-2,000		2,001-4,000		More than 4,000			
Survey question/responses	**Freq.**	**%**	**Freq.**	**%**	**Freq.**	**%**	**Freq.**	**%**	**Freq.**	**%**	**Freq.**	**%**	**Freq.**	**%**	**Freq.**	**%**	**Freq.**	**%**	**Freq.**	**%**
Q78. Please indicate each student outcome that was measured: (Select all that apply): *(cont.)*																				
Information literacy	16	17.8	88	25.1	50	22.3	54	25.0	29	22.0	27	27.6	24	26.1	15	22.1	9	18.0	104	23.6
Involvement in service	1	1.1	53	15.1	18	8.0	36	16.7	21	15.9	13	13.3	11	12.0	5	7.4	4	8.0	54	12.3
Out-of-class student-faculty interaction	8	8.9	102	29.1	53	23.7	57	26.4	26	19.7	27	27.6	26	28.3	12	17.6	19	38.0	110	25.0
Participation in campus activities	19	21.1	134	38.3	83	37.1	70	32.4	43	32.6	36	36.7	33	35.9	23	33.8	18	36.0	153	34.8
Persistence to graduation	25	27.8	89	25.4	74	33.0	40	18.5	31	23.5	16	16.3	27	29.3	21	30.9	19	38.0	114	25.9
Persistence to second year	56	62.2	201	57.4	153	68.3	104	48.1	68	51.5	49	50.0	62	67.4	46	67.6	32	64.0	257	58.4
Satisfaction with advising	18	20.0	96	27.4	49	21.9	65	30.1	38	28.8	25	25.5	24	26.1	18	26.5	9	18.0	114	25.9
Satisfaction with faculty	39	43.3	193	55.1	105	46.9	127	58.8	79	59.8	50	51.0	48	52.2	32	47.1	23	46.0	232	52.7
Satisfaction with the seminar	56	62.2	278	79.4	166	74.1	168	77.8	102	77.3	77	78.6	71	77.2	45	66.2	39	78.0	334	75.9
Satisfaction with the institution	18	20.0	126	36.0	62	27.7	82	38.0	49	37.1	30	30.6	33	35.9	16	23.5	16	32.0	144	32.7
Student self-reports of course impact	33	36.7	184	52.6	115	51.3	102	47.2	61	46.2	50	51.0	46	50.0	31	45.6	29	58.0	217	49.3
Student self-reports of improvement	24	26.7	115	32.9	74	33.0	65	30.1	35	26.5	30	30.6	30	32.6	27	39.7	17	34.0	139	31.6
Understanding of institutional identity and culture	10	11.1	65	18.6	31	13.8	44	20.4	25	18.9	15	15.3	20	21.7	9	13.2	6	12.0	75	17.0
Use of campus services	24	26.7	115	32.9	81	36.2	58	26.9	31	23.5	27	27.6	36	39.1	26	38.2	19	38.0	139	31.6
Writing ability	14	15.6	87	24.9	32	14.3	69	31.9	35	26.5	28	28.6	22	23.9	11	16.2	5	10.0	101	23.0
Other (please specify)	3	3.3	26	7.4	14	6.3	15	6.9	8	6.1	7	7.1	6	6.5	4	5.9	4	8.0	29	6.6
Total	90	100.0	350	100.0	224	100.0	216	100.0	132	100.0	98	100.0	92	100.0	68	100.0	50	100.0	440	100.0

All Responses by Seminar Type

Survey question/responses	Extended orientation seminar		Academic seminar: uniform content		Academic seminar: various topics		Preprofessional or discipline-linked seminar		Basic study skills seminar		Hybrid	
	Freq.	%	Freq.	%	Freq.	%	Freq.	%	Freq.	%	Freq.	%
Q17. What is the approximate percentage of first-year students who take a first-year seminar on your campus?												
Less than 10%	21	6.8	10	6.7	4	2.6	4	13.3	6	19.4	4	3.6
10-19%	18	5.9	7	4.7	8	5.3	5	16.7	3	9.7	6	5.4
20-29%	22	7.2	4	2.7	7	4.6	3	10.0	3	9.7	8	7.2
30-39%	15	4.9	1	0.7	7	4.6	1	3.3	3	9.7	7	6.3
40-49%	13	4.2	5	3.4	5	3.3	3	10.0	1	3.2	2	1.8
50-59%	17	5.5	11	7.4	3	2.0	0	0.0	4	12.9	3	2.7
60-69%	12	3.9	5	3.4	3	2.0	0	0.0	3	9.7	5	4.5
70-79%	24	7.8	8	5.4	6	4.0	2	6.7	1	3.2	3	2.7
80-89%	27	8.8	9	6.0	5	3.3	2	6.7	1	3.2	6	5.4
90-99%	68	22.1	36	24.2	19	12.6	3	10.0	2	6.5	21	18.9
100%	70	22.8	53	35.6	84	55.6	7	23.3	4	12.9	46	41.4
Total	307	100.0	149	100.0	151	100.0	30	100.0	31	100.0	111	100.0
Q18. Approximately how many years has a first-year seminar been offered on your campus?												
2 years or less	34	11.1	8	5.4	6	4.0	2	6.7	3	9.7	7	6.3
3-5 years	45	14.7	30	20.1	24	15.9	9	30.0	11	35.5	15	13.5
6-10 years	72	23.5	43	28.9	34	22.5	7	23.3	7	22.6	37	33.3
11-15 years	59	19.2	20	13.4	30	19.9	5	16.7	2	6.5	22	19.8
16-20 years	45	14.7	18	12.1	24	15.9	0	0.0	5	16.1	17	15.3
More than 20 years	52	16.9	30	20.1	33	21.9	7	23.3	3	9.7	13	11.7
Total	307	100.0	149	100.0	151	100.0	30	100.0	31	100.0	111	100.0

Survey question/responses	Extended orientation seminar		Academic seminar: uniform content		Academic seminar: various topics		Preprofessional or discipline-linked seminar		Basic study skills seminar		Hybrid	
	Freq.	%	Freq.	%	Freq.	%	Freq.	%	Freq.	%	Freq.	%
Q19. Which of the following types of first-year seminars does your institution currently offer?												
Extended orientation seminar	306	99.7	62	41.6	40	26.5	22	73.3	13	41.9	28	25.2
Academic seminar - uniform content	40	13.0	138	92.6	20	13.2	8	26.7	9	29.0	17	15.3
Academic seminar - various topics	25	8.1	25	16.8	137	90.7	13	43.3	8	25.8	15	13.5
Preprofessional or discipline-linked seminar	44	14.3	22	14.8	18	11.9	29	96.7	4	12.9	12	10.8
Basic study skills seminar	63	20.5	40	26.8	14	9.3	14	46.7	31	100.0	14	12.6
Hybrid	35	11.4	11	7.4	17	11.3	3	10.0	7	22.6	109	98.2
Other	5	1.6	2	1.3	2	1.3	0	0.0	0	0.0	1	0.9
Total	307	100.0	149	100.0	151	100.0	30	100.0	31	100.0	111	100.0
Q23. Please indicate the approximate number of sections of this seminar type that will be offered in the 2012-2013 academic year:												
1-10 sections	63	20.5	38	25.5	14	9.3	14	46.7	12	38.7	24	21.6
11-20 sections	72	23.5	40	26.8	27	17.9	3	10.0	7	22.6	35	31.5
21-30 sections	55	17.9	27	18.1	36	23.8	5	16.7	6	19.4	22	19.8
31-40 sections	26	8.5	11	7.4	25	16.6	4	13.3	1	3.2	10	9.0
41-50 sections	27	8.8	9	6.0	17	11.3	0	0.0	2	6.5	8	7.2
More than 50 sections	64	20.8	24	16.1	32	21.2	4	13.3	3	9.7	12	10.8
Total	307	100.0	149	100.0	151	100.0	30	100.0	31	100.0	111	100.0
Q24. What is the approximate class size for each first-year seminar section?												
Fewer than 10 students	1	0.3	2	1.3	1	0.7	1	3.3	0	0.0	0	0.0
10-14 students	25	8.2	11	7.4	11	7.4	1	3.3	2	6.5	11	9.9
15-19 students	81	26.5	54	36.2	89	59.7	6	20.0	9	29.0	41	36.9
20-24 students	111	36.3	52	34.9	36	24.2	5	16.7	15	48.4	39	35.1
25-29 students	57	18.6	17	11.4	9	6.0	2	6.7	5	16.1	14	12.6
More than 30 students	31	10.1	13	8.7	3	2.0	15	50.0	0	0.0	6	5.4
Total	306	100.0	149	100.0	149	100.0	30	100.0	31	100.0	111	100.0

Table continues p. 110

Table continued from p. 109

Survey question/responses	Extended orientation seminar		Academic seminar: uniform content		Academic seminar: various topics		Preprofessional or discipline-linked seminar		Basic study skills seminar		Hybrid	
	Freq.	%	Freq.	%	Freq.	%	Freq.	%	Freq.	%	Freq.	%
Q25. What is the approximate percentage of first-year students required to take the first-year seminar?												
None are required to take it	55	18.0	22	14.8	30	20.1	5	16.7	4	12.9	15	13.5
Less than 10%	18	5.9	4	2.7	3	2.0	4	13.3	8	25.8	2	1.8
10-19%	16	5.2	4	2.7	3	2.0	3	10.0	2	6.5	7	6.3
20-29%	8	2.6	3	2.0	2	1.3	1	3.3	4	12.9	6	5.4
30-39%	8	2.6	2	1.3	2	1.3	1	3.3	1	3.2	1	0.9
40-49%	4	1.3	4	2.7	1	0.7	0	0.0	2	6.5	0	0.0
50-59%	8	2.6	4	2.7	0	0.0	0	0.0	3	9.7	3	2.7
60-69%	5	1.6	5	3.4	0	0.0	0	0.0	0	0.0	3	2.7
70-79%	15	4.9	5	3.4	2	1.3	3	10.0	0	0.0	1	0.9
80-89%	14	4.6	8	5.4	2	1.3	1	3.3	1	3.2	5	4.5
90-99%	48	15.7	27	18.1	11	7.4	0	0.0	2	6.5	17	15.3
100%	107	35.0	61	40.9	93	62.4	12	40.0	4	12.9	51	45.9
Total	306	100.0	149	100.0	149	100.0	30	100.0	31	100.0	111	100.0
Q26. Which students, by category, are required to take the first-year seminar?												
All first-year students are required to take it	162	64.8	89	70.6	100	84.7	10	40.0	7	25.9	65	67.7
Academically underprepared students	34	13.6	16	12.7	2	1.7	4	16.0	14	51.9	10	10.4
First-generation students	4	1.6	7	5.6	2	1.7	1	4.0	0	0.0	2	2.1
Honors students	3	1.2	2	1.6	2	1.7	3	12.0	0	0.0	3	3.1
International students	4	1.6	1	0.8	1	0.8	0	0.0	0	0.0	4	4.2
Learning community participants	10	4.0	3	2.4	4	3.4	5	20.0	4	14.8	5	5.2

Survey question/responses	Extended orientation seminar		Academic seminar: uniform content		Academic seminar: various topics		Preprofessional or discipline-linked seminar		Basic study skills seminar		Hybrid	
	Freq.	%	Freq.	%	Freq.	%	Freq.	%	Freq.	%	Freq.	%
Q26. Which students, by category, are required to take the first-year seminar? *(cont.)*												
Preprofessional students (e.g., prelaw, premed)	4	1.6	2	1.6	1	0.8	6	24.0	0	0.0	1	1.0
Provisionally admitted students	12	4.8	8	6.3	5	4.2	1	4.0	2	7.4	4	4.2
Student athletes	12	4.8	5	4.0	0	0.0	1	4.0	1	3.7	3	3.1
Students enrolled in developmental or remedial courses	21	8.4	7	5.6	1	0.8	0	0.0	12	44.4	5	5.2
Students participating in dual-enrollment programs	1	0.4	1	0.8	1	0.8	0	0.0	0	0.0	0	0.0
Students residing within a particular residence hall	3	1.2	1	0.8	0	0.0	1	4.0	0	0.0	0	0.0
Transfer students	3	1.2	1	0.8	2	1.7	0	0.0	0	0.0	0	0.0
TRIO participants	7	2.8	5	4.0	2	1.7	2	8.0	4	14.8	3	3.1
Undeclared students	6	2.4	3	2.4	1	0.8	2	8.0	1	3.7	4	4.2
Students within specific majors (please specify)	16	6.4	11	8.7	6	5.1	8	32.0	3	11.1	7	7.3
Other (please specify)	28	11.2	12	9.5	6	5.1	1	4.0	2	7.4	16	16.7
Total	250	100.0	126	100.0	118	100.0	25	100.0	27	100.0	96	100.0
Q27. Please identify unique subpopulations of students for which special sections of the first-year seminar are offered:												
No special sections are offered	105	34.4	61	41.2	69	46.6	9	30.0	12	38.7	44	39.6
Academically underprepared students	52	17.0	31	20.9	18	12.2	9	30.0	6	19.4	14	12.6
First-generation students	15	4.9	7	4.7	11	7.4	1	3.3	1	3.2	6	5.4
Honors students	70	23.0	37	25.0	39	26.4	8	26.7	4	12.9	30	27.0
International students	21	6.9	4	2.7	12	8.1	3	10.0	3	9.7	10	9.0
Learning community participants	65	21.3	26	17.6	26	17.6	9	30.0	5	16.1	16	14.4

Table continues p. 112

Table continued from p. 111

Survey question/responses	Extended orientation seminar		Academic seminar: uniform content		Academic seminar: various topics		Preprofessional or discipline-linked seminar		Basic study skills seminar		Hybrid	
	Freq.	%	Freq.	%	Freq.	%	Freq.	%	Freq.	%	Freq.	%
Q27. Please identify unique subpopulations of students for which special sections of the first-year seminar are offered: *(cont.)*												
Preprofessional students (e.g., prelaw, premed)	32	10.5	10	6.8	3	2.0	7	23.3	1	3.2	7	6.3
Provisionally admitted students	19	6.2	10	6.8	3	2.0	2	6.7	2	6.5	2	1.8
Student athletes	39	12.8	9	6.1	4	2.7	3	10.0	2	6.5	3	2.7
Students enrolled in developmental or remedial courses	22	7.2	11	7.4	2	1.4	3	10.0	4	12.9	3	2.7
Students participating in dual-enrollment programs	5	1.6	3	2.0	2	1.4	0	0.0	1	3.2	1	0.9
Students residing within a particular residence hall	11	3.6	2	1.4	9	6.1	3	10.0	2	6.5	2	1.8
Transfer students	32	10.5	11	7.4	7	4.7	2	6.7	0	0.0	6	5.4
TRIO participants	17	5.6	10	6.8	4	2.7	4	13.3	4	12.9	5	4.5
Undeclared students	40	13.1	10	6.8	5	3.4	8	26.7	2	6.5	7	6.3
Students within specific majors (please specify)	51	16.7	18	12.2	16	10.8	9	30.0	3	9.7	14	12.6
Other (please specify)	45	14.8	13	8.8	8	5.4	1	3.3	1	3.2	15	13.5
Total	305	100.0	148	100.0	148	100.0	30	100.0	31	100.0	111	100.0
Q28. Who teaches the first-year seminar?												
Adjunct faculty	152	50.0	87	58.8	78	52.7	10	33.3	27	87.1	48	43.2
Full-time non-tenure-track faculty	161	53.0	95	64.2	108	73.0	12	40.0	19	61.3	74	66.7
Tenure-track faculty	192	63.2	100	67.6	135	91.2	25	83.3	13	41.9	86	77.5
Student affairs professionals	215	70.7	71	48.0	38	25.7	8	26.7	13	41.9	55	49.5
Other campus professionals (please specify)	118	38.8	41	27.7	34	23.0	7	23.3	6	19.4	40	36.0
Graduate students	19	6.3	3	2.0	3	2.0	4	13.3	1	3.2	6	5.4
Undergraduate students	18	5.9	0	0.0	2	1.4	3	10.0	0	0.0	8	7.2
Total	304	100.0	148	100.0	148	100.0	30	100.0	31	100.0	111	100.0

Survey question/responses	Extended orientation seminar		Academic seminar: uniform content		Academic seminar: various topics		Preprofessional or discipline-linked seminar		Basic study skills seminar		Hybrid	
	Freq.	%	Freq.	%	Freq.	%	Freq.	%	Freq.	%	Freq.	%
Q29. Faculty who teach the first-year seminar teach the course as which of the following?												
Part of regular teaching load	153	61.0	112	79.4	133	91.7	21	84.0	27	87.1	70	73.7
An additional course beyond regular teaching load	161	64.1	60	42.6	41	28.3	7	28.0	15	48.4	43	45.3
Other (please specify)	13	5.2	8	5.7	5	3.4	0	0.0	2	6.5	7	7.4
Total	251	100.0	141	100.0	145	100.0	25	100.0	31	100.0	95	100.0
Q30. Staff (student affairs and other campus professionals) who teach the first-year seminar teach the course as which of the following?												
An assigned responsibility	93	41.9	37	42.5	12	21.8	6	66.7	4	23.5	30	45.5
An extra responsibility	161	72.5	66	75.9	46	83.6	5	55.6	12	70.6	41	62.1
Other (please specify)	24	10.8	12	13.8	8	14.5	0	0.0	3	17.6	16	24.2
Total	222	100.0	87	100.0	55	100.0	9	100.0	17	100.0	66	100.0
Q31. Graduate students who teach the first-year seminar teach the course as which of the following?												
An assigned responsibility	9	60.0	3	100.0	0	0.0	3	100.0	0	0.0	2	40.0
An extra responsibility	4	26.7	1	33.3	2	66.7	0	0.0	1	100.0	3	60.0
Other (please specify)	3	20.0	0	0.0	1	33.3	0	0.0	0	0.0	1	20.0
Total	15	100.0	3	100.0	3	100.0	3	100.0	1	100.0	5	100.0
Q32. If the first-year seminar is taught as an additional course or as an extra responsibility, what type of compensation is offered for teaching a first-year seminar?												
Direct monetary compensation or stipend	177	88.1	75	88.2	54	79.4	5	45.5	18	90.0	53	86.9
Graduate student support	3	1.5	2	2.4	0	0.0	1	9.1	0	0.0	0	0.0
Professional development funds	6	3.0	2	2.4	5	7.4	0	0.0	0	0.0	3	4.9
Release time	16	8.0	6	7.1	8	11.8	0	0.0	1	5.0	1	1.6
No additional compensation	30	14.9	6	7.1	12	17.6	5	45.5	1	5.0	10	16.4
Other (please specify)	8	4.0	5	5.9	7	10.3	1	9.1	1	5.0	4	6.6
Total	201	100.0	85	100.0	68	100.0	11	100.0	20	100.0	61	100.0

Table continues p. 114

Table continued from p. 113

Survey question/responses	Extended orientation seminar		Academic seminar: uniform content		Academic seminar: various topics		Preprofessional or discipline-linked seminar		Basic study skills seminar		Hybrid	
	Freq.	%	Freq.	%	Freq.	%	Freq.	%	Freq.	%	Freq.	%
Q37. Is instructor training offered for first-year seminar instructors?												
I don't know	5	1.7	2	1.4	7	4.7	5	16.7	1	3.4	0	0.0
Yes	248	83.5	130	87.8	111	75.0	17	56.7	20	69.0	96	88.1
No	44	14.8	16	10.8	30	20.3	8	26.7	8	27.6	13	11.9
Total	297	100.0	148	100.0	148	100.0	30	100.0	29	100.0	109	100.0
Q38. Is instructor training required for first-year seminar instructors?												
Yes	188	76.1	101	77.7	57	51.4	7	41.2	16	84.2	63	66.3
No	57	23.1	27	20.8	52	46.8	10	58.8	3	15.8	31	32.6
I don't know	2	0.8	2	1.5	2	1.8	0	0.0	0	0.0	1	1.1
Total	247	100.0	130	100.0	111	100.0	17	100.0	19	100.0	95	100.0
Q39. How long is the initial instructor training?												
Half a day or less	114	46.2	38	29.2	38	34.2	9	52.9	9	47.4	40	42.1
1 day	61	24.7	36	27.7	37	33.3	2	11.8	5	26.3	18	18.9
2 days	29	11.7	19	14.6	15	13.5	3	17.6	3	15.8	10	10.5
3 days	10	4.0	4	3.1	5	4.5	2	11.8	1	5.3	4	4.2
4 days	4	1.6	6	4.6	1	0.9	0	0.0	0	0.0	3	3.2
1 week	7	2.8	8	6.2	5	4.5	0	0.0	0	0.0	4	4.2
2 weeks	1	0.4	1	0.8	1	0.9	0	0.0	0	0.0	2	2.1
Other (please specify)	21	8.5	18	13.8	9	8.1	1	5.9	1	5.3	14	14.7
Total	247	100.0	130	100.0	111	100.0	17	100.0	19	100.0	95	100.0
Q40. Is there ongoing instructor development after initial training?												
Yes (please explain)	178	72.1	100	76.9	93	83.8	13	76.5	11	57.9	72	75.8
No	69	27.9	30	23.1	18	16.2	4	23.5	8	42.1	23	24.2
Total	247	100.0	130	100.0	111	100.0	17	100.0	19	100.0	95	100.0

Survey question/responses	Extended orientation seminar		Academic seminar: uniform content		Academic seminar: various topics		Preprofessional or discipline-linked seminar		Basic study skills seminar		Hybrid	
	Freq.	%	Freq.	%	Freq.	%	Freq.	%	Freq.	%	Freq.	%
Q41. If undergraduate students assist in the first year seminar, what is their primary role?												
They teach independently	6	2.0	1	0.7	4	2.7	2	6.9	1	3.6	3	2.8
They teach as a part of a team	55	18.6	8	5.4	9	6.1	4	13.8	2	7.1	17	15.7
They assist the instructor, but do not teach	76	25.7	43	29.1	41	27.7	7	24.1	5	17.9	33	30.6
Other (please specify)	36	12.2	22	14.9	33	22.3	2	6.9	2	7.1	18	16.7
Undergraduate students do not assist in the seminar	164	55.4	87	58.8	69	46.6	17	58.6	20	71.4	49	45.4
Total	296	100.0	148	100.0	148	100.0	29	100.0	20	100.0	108	100.0
Q42. Please indicate the approximate percentage of sections that are team taught:												
No sections are team taught	156	52.7	83	56.1	67	45.3	14	48.3	20	71.4	55	50.9
Less than 10%	58	19.6	38	25.7	54	36.5	8	27.6	5	17.9	21	19.4
10-19%	8	2.7	8	5.4	11	7.4	2	6.9	1	3.6	8	7.4
20-29%	9	3.0	3	2.0	1	0.7	1	3.4	1	3.6	0	0.0
30-39%	5	1.7	2	1.4	1	0.7	1	3.4	0	0.0	2	1.9
40-49%	0	0.0	1	0.7	0	0.0	1	3.4	0	0.0	0	0.0
50-59%	6	2.0	1	0.7	1	0.7	1	3.4	0	0.0	0	0.0
60-69%	0	0.0	1	0.7	0	0.0	0	0.0	0	0.0	1	0.9
70-79%	3	1.0	0	0.0	2	1.4	0	0.0	0	0.0	0	0.0
80-89%	2	0.7	0	0.0	1	0.7	0	0.0	0	0.0	2	1.9
90-99%	3	1.0	4	2.7	2	1.4	0	0.0	0	0.0	3	2.8
100%	46	15.5	7	4.7	8	5.4	1	3.4	1	3.6	16	14.8
Total	296	100.0	148	100.0	148	100.0	29	100.0	28	100.0	108	100.0

Table continues p. 116

Table continued from p. 117

	Extended orientation seminar		Academic seminar: uniform content		Academic seminar: various topics		Preprofessional or discipline-linked seminar		Basic study skills seminar		Hybrid	
Survey question/responses	**Freq.**	**%**	**Freq.**	**%**	**Freq.**	**%**	**Freq.**	**%**	**Freq.**	**%**	**Freq.**	**%**
Q44. What is the approximate percentage of students placed in sections with their academic advisors?												
No students are placed in sections with their academic advisors	111	37.5	57	38.5	54	36.7	8	27.6	20	71.4	39	36.1
Less than 10%	55	18.6	23	15.5	16	10.9	8	27.6	4	14.3	14	13.0
10-19%	18	6.1	11	7.4	3	2.0	3	10.3	0	0.0	4	3.7
20-29%	19	6.4	6	4.1	5	3.4	0	0.0	0	0.0	2	1.9
30-39%	4	1.4	6	4.1	6	4.1	0	0.0	0	0.0	2	1.9
40-49%	1	0.3	1	0.7	0	0.0	0	0.0	1	3.6	1	0.9
50-59%	8	2.7	3	2.0	3	2.0	0	0.0	0	0.0	2	1.9
60-69%	1	0.3	1	0.7	3	2.0	0	0.0	0	0.0	2	1.9
70-79%	3	1.0	1	0.7	3	2.0	1	3.4	0	0.0	0	0.0
80-89%	8	2.7	1	0.7	4	2.7	0	0.0	0	0.0	0	0.0
90-99%	10	3.4	3	2.0	5	3.4	2	6.9	0	0.0	5	4.6
100%	27	9.1	21	14.2	28	19.0	2	6.9	2	7.1	21	19.4
I don't know	30	10.1	14	9.5	17	11.6	5	17.2	1	3.6	16	14.8
Total	296	100.0	148	100.0	147	100.0	29	100.0	28	100.0	108	100.0
Q45. What is the typical duration of a section of the first-year seminar?												
Half a term	44	14.9	19	12.8	2	1.4	3	10.3	1	3.6	7	6.5
One quarter	6	2.0	5	3.4	6	4.1	1	3.4	1	3.6	2	1.9
One semester	205	69.3	105	70.9	117	79.6	22	75.9	26	92.9	77	71.3
One year	11	3.7	9	6.1	12	8.2	2	6.9	0	0.0	8	7.4
Other (please specify)	30	10.1	10	6.8	10	6.8	1	3.4	0	0.0	14	13.0
Total	296	100.0	148	100.0	147	100.0	29	100.0	28	100.0	108	100.0

Survey question/responses	Extended orientation seminar		Academic seminar: uniform content		Academic seminar: various topics		Preprofessional or discipline-linked seminar		Basic study skills seminar		Hybrid	
	Freq.	%	Freq.	%	Freq.	%	Freq.	%	Freq.	%	Freq.	%
Q46. How many total classroom contact hours are there per week in the first-year seminar?												
1 hour	129	43.6	31	20.9	17	11.6	16	55.2	4	14.3	30	27.8
2 hours	81	27.4	33	22.3	14	9.5	8	27.6	12	42.9	20	18.5
3 hours	78	26.4	70	47.3	88	59.9	4	13.8	12	42.9	39	36.1
4 hours	3	1.0	6	4.1	26	17.7	0	0.0	0	0.0	15	13.9
5 hours	1	0.3	2	1.4	1	0.7	0	0.0	0	0.0	0	0.0
6 or more hours	4	1.4	6	4.1	1	0.7	1	3.4	0	0.0	4	3.7
Total	296	100.0	148	100.0	147	100.0	29	100.0	28	100.0	108	100.0
Q47. Does the first-year seminar carry academic credit?												
Yes	275	92.9	142	95.9	144	98.0	25	86.2	26	92.9	104	96.3
No	21	7.1	6	4.1	3	2.0	4	13.8	2	7.1	4	3.7
Total	296	100.0	148	100.0	147	100.0	29	100.0	28	100.0	108	100.0
Q48. How many credits does the first-year seminar carry?												
1 credit	168	61.3	50	35.2	24	16.7	19	76.0	8	30.8	43	41.3
2 credits	35	12.8	16	11.3	9	6.3	3	12.0	6	23.1	13	12.5
3 credits	70	25.5	59	41.5	52	36.1	3	12.0	12	46.2	30	28.8
4 credits	0	0.0	7	4.9	52	36.1	0	0.0	0	0.0	17	16.3
5 credits	1	0.4	1	0.7	1	0.7	0	0.0	0	0.0	0	0.0
6 or more credits	0	0.0	9	6.3	6	4.2	0	0.0	0	0.0	1	1.0
Total	274	100.0	142	100.0	144	100.0	25	100.0	26	100.0	104	100.0
Q49. How is the first-year seminar credit applied?												
As an elective	133	48.5	42	29.6	35	24.3	15	60.0	16	61.5	30	28.8
Toward general education requirements	129	47.1	99	69.7	111	77.1	7	28.0	7	26.9	67	64.4
Toward major requirements	19	6.9	10	7.0	18	12.5	8	32.0	1	3.8	5	4.8
Other (please specify)	23	8.4	11	7.7	20	13.9	4	16.0	4	15.4	17	16.3
Total	274	100.0	142	100.0	144	100.0	25	100.0	26	100.0	104	100.0

Table continues p. 118

Table continued from p. 117

Survey question/responses	Extended orientation seminar		Academic seminar: uniform content		Academic seminar: various topics		Preprofessional or discipline-linked seminar		Basic study skills seminar		Hybrid	
	Freq.	%	Freq.	%	Freq.	%	Freq.	%	Freq.	%	Freq.	%
Q50. How is the first-year seminar graded?												
Letter grade	235	79.7	133	89.9	138	93.9	19	65.5	25	89.3	93	86.1
Pass/fail	50	16.9	15	10.1	5	3.4	8	27.6	3	10.7	12	11.1
No grade	7	2.4	0	0.0	0	0.0	1	3.4	0	0.0	0	0.0
Other (please specify)	3	1.0	2	1.4	4	2.7	1	3.4	0	0.0	3	2.8
Total	295	100.0	148	100.0	147	100.0	29	100.0	28	100.0	108	100.0
Q51. Do any sections incorporate online components?												
I don't know	16	5.4	9	6.1	22	15.0	9	31.0	1	3.6	5	4.6
Yes	193	65.4	94	63.5	66	44.9	13	44.8	19	67.9	67	62.0
No	86	29.2	45	30.4	59	40.1	7	24.1	8	28.6	36	33.3
Total	295	100.0	148	100.0	147	100.0	29	100.0	28	100.0	108	100.0
Q53. Are there any online-only sections?												
Yes	76	39.4	29	30.9	5	7.6	4	30.8	9	47.4	15	22.4
No	114	59.1	65	69.1	60	90.9	9	69.2	10	52.6	52	77.6
I don't know	3	1.6	0	0.0	1	1.5	0	0.0	0	0.0	0	0.0
Total	193	100.0	94	100.0	66	100.0	13	100.0	19	100.0	67	100.0
Q54. Please indicate the approximate percentage of online-only sections:												
Less than 10%	42	55.3	14	48.3	2	40.0	4	100.0	3	33.3	10	71.4
10-19%	13	17.1	7	24.1	2	40.0	0	0.0	2	22.2	0	0.0
20-29%	10	13.2	3	10.3	1	20.0	0	0.0	1	11.1	2	14.3
30-39%	2	2.6	3	10.3	0	0.0	0	0.0	2	22.2	1	7.1
40-49%	4	5.3	0	0.0	0	0.0	0	0.0	0	0.0	0	0.0
50-59%	0	0.0	1	3.4	0	0.0	0	0.0	1	11.1	0	0.0
60-69%	1	1.3	0	0.0	0	0.0	0	0.0	0	0.0	0	0.0
70 - 79%	0	0.0	0	0.0	0	0.0	0	0.0	0	0.0	0	0.0
80-89%	0	0.0	0	0.0	0	0.0	0	0.0	0	0.0	1	7.1
90-99%	1	1.3	0	0.0	0	0.0	0	0.0	0	0.0	0	0.0
100%	3	3.9	1	3.4	0	0.0	0	0.0	0	0.0	0	0.0
Total	76	100.0	29	100.0	5	100.0	4	100.0	9	100.0	14	100.0

Survey question/responses	Extended orientation seminar		Academic seminar: uniform content		Academic seminar: various topics		Preprofessional or discipline-linked seminar		Basic study skills seminar		Hybrid	
	Freq.	%	Freq.	%	Freq.	%	Freq.	%	Freq.	%	Freq.	%
Q55. Select the three most important course objectives for the first year seminar:												
Create common first-year experience	58	19.7	53	35.8	26	17.7	4	13.8	3	10.7	19	17.8
Develop a connection with the institution	166	56.3	54	36.5	46	31.3	12	41.4	8	28.6	53	49.5
Develop academic skills	102	34.6	56	37.8	47	32.0	6	20.7	13	46.4	49	45.8
Develop critical-thinking skills	23	7.8	46	31.1	74	50.3	5	17.2	5	17.9	22	20.6
Develop financial literacy	9	3.1	2	1.4	0	0.0	0	0.0	1	3.6	0	0.0
Develop information literacy	17	5.8	14	9.5	15	10.2	2	6.9	2	7.1	5	4.7
Develop oral communication skills	2	0.7	3	2.0	24	16.3	1	3.4	0	0.0	2	1.9
Develop study skills	81	27.5	30	20.3	7	4.8	2	6.9	19	67.9	13	12.1
Develop support network or friendships	58	19.7	21	14.2	12	8.2	4	13.8	2	7.1	12	11.2
Develop writing skills	2	0.7	20	13.5	57	38.8	0	0.0	1	3.6	7	6.5
Develop intercultural competence	1	0.3	3	2.0	0	0.0	0	0.0	0	0.0	2	1.9
Improve second-year return rates	59	20.0	15	10.1	11	7.5	2	6.9	4	14.3	18	16.8
Increase student-faculty interaction	21	7.1	14	9.5	36	24.5	5	17.2	2	7.1	15	14.0
Introduce a discipline	4	1.4	2	1.4	14	9.5	14	48.3	0	0.0	4	3.7
Introduce the liberal arts	5	1.7	21	14.2	24	16.3	2	6.9	0	0.0	11	10.3
Provide orientation to campus resources and services	172	58.3	40	27.0	17	11.6	6	20.7	14	50.0	37	34.6
Provide career exploration	30	10.2	8	5.4	2	1.4	4	13.8	2	7.1	2	1.9
Provide preprofessional preparation	1	0.3	0	0.0	2	1.4	12	41.4	0	0.0	0	0.0
Self-exploration or personal development	56	19.0	24	16.2	4	2.7	3	10.3	8	28.6	30	28.0
Other (please specify)	13	4.4	15	10.1	17	11.6	2	6.9	0	0.0	15	14.0
Total	295	100.0	148	100.0	147	100.0	29	100.0	28	100.0	107	100.0

Table continues p. 120

Table continued from p. 119

Survey question/responses	Extended orientation seminar		Academic seminar: uniform content		Academic seminar: various topics		Preprofessional or discipline-linked seminar		Basic study skills seminar		Hybrid	
	Freq.	%	Freq.	%	Freq.	%	Freq.	%	Freq.	%	Freq.	%
Q56. Select the three most important topics that compose the content of this first-year seminar:												
Academic planning or advising	139	47.1	52	35.1	18	12.2	12	41.4	8	28.6	34	31.8
Career exploration or preparation	60	20.3	30	20.3	7	4.8	13	44.8	7	25.0	13	12.1
Campus engagement	97	32.9	41	27.7	22	15.0	4	13.8	6	21.4	37	34.6
Campus resources	166	56.3	35	23.6	13	8.8	11	37.9	13	46.4	33	30.8
College policies and procedures	53	18.0	16	10.8	4	2.7	6	20.7	3	10.7	11	10.3
Critical thinking	32	10.8	68	45.9	93	63.3	6	20.7	5	17.9	40	37.4
Diversity issues	13	4.4	6	4.1	5	3.4	3	10.3	1	3.6	6	5.6
Financial literacy	14	4.7	2	1.4	1	0.7	0	0.0	0	0.0	1	0.9
Global learning	0	0.0	6	4.1	14	9.5	0	0.0	0	0.0	5	4.7
Health and wellness	5	1.7	3	2.0	1	0.7	0	0.0	1	3.6	1	0.9
Information literacy	22	7.5	19	12.8	21	14.3	4	13.8	4	14.3	5	4.7
Oral communication skills	2	0.7	8	5.4	21	14.3	2	6.9	0	0.0	6	5.6
Relationship issues (e.g., interpersonal skills, conflict resolution)	27	9.2	11	7.4	4	2.7	1	3.4	4	14.3	10	9.3
Specific disciplinary topic	1	0.3	15	10.1	49	33.3	13	44.8	0	0.0	22	20.6
Study skills	116	39.3	36	24.3	16	10.9	5	17.2	19	67.9	33	30.8
Time management	95	32.2	31	20.9	6	4.1	3	10.3	12	42.9	25	23.4
Writing skills	10	3.4	35	23.6	72	49.0	0	0.0	0	0.0	14	13.1
Other (please specify)	22	7.5	25	16.9	33	22.4	3	10.3	1	3.6	21	19.6
Total	295	100.0	148	100.0	147	100.0	29	100.0	28	100.0	107	100.0

Survey question/responses	Extended orientation seminar		Academic seminar: uniform content		Academic seminar: various topics		Preprofessional or discipline-linked seminar		Basic study skills seminar		Hybrid	
	Freq.	%	Freq.	%	Freq.	%	Freq.	%	Freq.	%	Freq.	%
Q57. Which of the following approaches associated with high-impact educational practices are intentionally incorporated into the first-year seminar? (Select all that apply):												
Writing-intensive experiences	75	25.5	81	54.7	105	71.4	7	24.1	8	28.6	45	42.1
Collaboration and teamwork	203	69.0	99	66.9	90	61.2	19	65.5	21	75.0	76	71.0
Diversity and global learning	162	55.1	99	66.9	84	57.1	15	51.7	11	39.3	72	67.3
None of the above	53	18.0	8	5.4	12	8.2	5	17.2	5	17.9	12	11.2
Total	294	100.0	148	100.0	147	100.0	29	100.0	28	100.0	107	100.0
Q59. Which of the following high-impact educational practices are connected to the first-year seminar? (Select all that apply):												
Service-Learning	83	28.6	48	33.3	55	37.7	7	24.1	7	25.0	36	33.6
Learning Community	107	36.9	56	38.9	55	37.7	13	44.8	9	32.1	35	32.7
Common Reading Experience	92	31.7	67	46.5	54	37.0	8	27.6	7	25.0	54	50.5
Undergraduate Research	18	6.2	14	9.7	40	27.4	5	17.2	1	3.6	17	15.9
None of the above	107	36.9	36	25.0	35	24.0	12	41.4	15	53.6	27	25.2
Total	290	100.0	144	100.0	146	100.0	29	100.0	28	100.0	107	100.0
Q60. How many total hours are students required to complete for the service-learning component?												
There is no requirement about the total number of hours.	27	32.9	10	37.5	33	60.0	3	42.9	2	28.6	17	47.2
5 or fewer	35	42.7	13	27.1	11	20.0	2	28.6	3	42.9	8	22.2
6-10	17	20.7	14	29.2	6	10.9	2	28.6	2	28.6	7	19.4
11-15	1	1.2	1	2.1	1	1.8	0	0.0	0	0.0	0	0.0
16-20	0	0.0	1	2.1	3	5.5	0	0.0	0	0.0	3	8.3
More than 20	2	2.4	1	2.1	1	1.8	0	0.0	0	0.0	1	2.8
Total	82	100.0	48	100.0	55	100.0	7	100.0	7	100.0	36	100.0

Table continues p. 122

Table continued from p. 121

Survey question/responses	Extended orientation seminar		Academic seminar: uniform content		Academic seminar: various topics		Preprofessional or discipline-linked seminar		Basic study skills seminar		Hybrid	
	Freq.	%	Freq.	%	Freq.	%	Freq.	%	Freq.	%	Freq.	%
Q61. Which of the following are used as reflection techniques in the first-year seminar associated with the service-learning component? (Select all that apply):												
Class discussion	62	75.6	40	83.3	39	70.9	5	71.4	6	85.7	31	86.1
Portfolio	11	13.4	14	29.2	9	16.4	3	42.9	4	57.1	6	16.7
Student presentations	33	40.2	30	62.5	27	49.1	4	57.1	3	42.9	21	58.3
Writing exercise, such as writing a paper or journaling	63	76.8	38	79.2	40	72.7	4	57.1	6	85.7	30	83.3
Other (please specify)	5	6.1	6	12.5	9	16.4	0	0.0	0	0.0	3	8.3
There is no reflection associated with the service-learning component.	6	7.3	2	4.2	2	3.6	1	14.3	0	0.0	0	0.0
Total	82	100.0	48	100.0	55	100.0	7	100.0	7	100.0	36	100.0
Q63. Which of the following are characteristics of the learning community of which the first-year seminar is a part? (Select all that apply):												
Co-enrollment, not all courses	87	82.1	35	62.5	36	65.5	9	69.2	7	77.8	29	82.9
Co-enrollment, all other courses	9	8.5	5	8.9	6	10.9	2	15.4	0	0.0	2	5.7
Coordinated course content	37	34.9	19	33.9	17	30.9	5	38.5	3	33.3	14	40.0
Course content connected by common intellectual theme	25	23.6	18	32.1	14	25.5	2	15.4	3	33.3	9	25.7
Common set of theme-based experiences outside of the course	29	27.4	23	41.1	18	32.7	6	46.2	2	22.2	14	40.0
Living-learning community	30	28.3	12	21.4	25	45.5	6	46.2	0	0.0	11	31.4
Other (please specify)	8	7.5	4	7.1	6	10.9	0	0.0	0	0.0	4	11.4
Total	106	100.0	56	100.0	55	100.0	13	100.0	9	100.0	35	100.0

Survey question/responses	Extended orientation seminar		Academic seminar: uniform content		Academic seminar: various topics		Preprofessional or discipline-linked seminar		Basic study skills seminar		Hybrid	
	Freq.	%	Freq.	%	Freq.	%	Freq.	%	Freq.	%	Freq.	%
Q67. What campus unit directly administors the first-year seminar?												
Academic affairs central office	59	20.4	41	28.5	61	41.8	4	14.3	5	17.9	24	22.4
College or school (e.g., College of Liberal Arts)	19	6.6	13	9.0	18	12.3	8	28.6	1	3.6	11	10.3
Academic department(s) (please specify)	58	20.1	32	22.2	18	12.3	8	28.6	12	42.9	21	19.6
First-year program office	54	18.7	27	18.8	14	9.6	3	10.7	1	3.6	20	18.7
Student affairs central office	39	13.5	10	6.9	3	2.1	1	3.6	2	7.1	1	0.9
Other (please specify)	60	20.8	21	14.6	32	21.9	4	14.3	7	25.0	30	28.0
Total	289	100.0	144	100.0	146	100.0	28	100.0	28	100.0	107	100.0
Q68. Which of the following best describes the institutional division where the first-year program office is housed?												
Academic Affairs	20	51.9	19	70.4	12	85.7	3	100.0	1	100.0	12	60.0
Student Affairs	14	25.9	6	22.2	1	7.1	0	0.0	0	0.0	3	15.0
Enrollment Management	7	13.0	1	3.7	0	0.0	0	0.0	0	0.0	0	0.0
Other (please specify)	5	9.3	1	3.7	1	7.1	0	0.0	0	0.0	5	25.0
Total	54	100.0	27	100.0	14	100.0	3	100.0	1	100.0	20	100.0
Q69. Is there a dean, director, or coordinator of the first-year seminar?												
Yes	241	83.4	117	81.3	114	78.1	12	42.9	19	67.9	92	86.0
No	41	14.2	26	18.1	31	21.2	15	53.6	9	32.1	14	13.1
I don't know	1	0.3	1	0.7	1	0.7	1	3.6	0	0.0	1	0.9
Total	289	100.0	144	100.0	146	100.0	28	100.0	28	100.0	107	100.0

Table continues p. 124

Table continued from p. 123

Survey question/responses	Extended orientation seminar		Academic seminar: uniform content		Academic seminar: various topics		Preprofessional or discipline-linked seminar		Basic study skills seminar		Hybrid	
	Freq.	**%**	**Freq.**	**%**	**Freq.**	**%**	**Freq.**	**%**	**Freq.**	**%**	**Freq.**	**%**
Q70. Does the dean, director, or coordinator of the first-year seminar work full time or less than full time in this position?												
Full time (approximately 40 hours a week)	119	49.4	58	49.6	34	29.8	9	75.0	11	57.9	30	32.6
Less than full time	122	50.6	59	50.4	80	70.2	3	25.0	8	42.1	62	67.4
Total	241	100.0	117	100.0	114	100.0	12	100.0	19	100.0	92	100.0
Q71. Does the dean, director, or coordinator have another position on campus?												
Yes	120	98.4	57	96.6	80	100.0	3	100.0	7	87.5	58	93.5
No	2	1.6	2	3.4	0	0.0	0	0.0	1	12.5	4	6.5
Total	122	100.0	59	100.0	80	100.0	3	100.0	8	100.0	62	100.0
Q72. The dean, director, or coordinator's other campus role is as which of the following? (Select all that apply):												
Academic affairs administrator	35	29.2	13	22.8	21	26.3	1	33.3	3	42.9	14	24.1
Faculty member	50	41.7	39	68.4	62	77.5	3	100.0	5	71.4	39	67.2
Student affairs administrator	30	25.0	9	15.8	3	3.8	0	0.0	0	0.0	7	12.1
Other (please specify)	18	15.0	8	14.0	6	7.5	0	0.0	0	0.0	12	20.7
Total	120	100.0	57	100.0	80	100.0	3	100.0	7	100.0	58	100.0
Q73. Has your first-year seminar been formally assessed or evaluated since fall 2009?												
Yes	177	61.2	83	57.6	84	57.5	15	53.6	11	39.3	70	65.4
No	82	28.4	55	38.2	53	36.3	10	35.7	11	39.3	30	28.0
I don't know	30	10.4	6	4.2	9	6.2	3	10.7	6	21.4	7	6.5
Total	289	100.0	144	100.0	146	100.0	28	100.0	28	100.0	107	100.0

Survey question/responses	Extended orientation seminar		Academic seminar: uniform content		Academic seminar: various topics		Preprofessional or discipline-linked seminar		Basic study skills seminar		Hybrid	
	Freq.	%	Freq.	%	Freq.	%	Freq.	%	Freq.	%	Freq.	%
Q74. What type of assessment was conducted? (Select all that apply):												
Analysis of institutional data (e.g., GPA, retention rates, graduation)	132	75.0	57	68.7	53	63.1	9	60.0	11	100.0	51	72.9
Direct assessment of student learning outcomes	80	45.5	50	60.2	46	54.8	10	66.7	6	54.5	43	61.4
Focus groups with instructors	61	34.7	37	44.6	25	29.8	2	13.3	4	36.4	26	37.1
Focus groups with students	50	28.4	34	41.0	26	31.0	2	13.3	2	18.2	21	30.0
Individual interviews with instructors	32	18.2	20	24.1	15	17.9	2	13.3	2	18.2	16	22.9
Individual interviews with students	21	11.9	14	16.9	7	8.3	3	20.0	1	9.1	9	12.9
Program review	59	33.5	31	37.3	24	28.6	5	33.3	5	45.5	24	34.3
Student course evaluation	152	86.4	74	89.2	71	84.5	11	73.3	10	90.9	65	92.9
Survey instrument	92	52.3	45	54.2	47	56.0	5	33.3	4	36.4	43	61.4
Total	176	100.0	83	100.0	84	100.0	15	100.0	11	100.0	70	100.0
Q75. What type of survey instrument did your institution use to assess or evaluate the first-year seminar? (Select all that apply):												
A locally developed (i.e., home-grown) survey of instructors	51	55.4	29	64.4	24	51.1	3	60.0	2	50.0	26	60.5
A locally developed survey of students	68	73.9	28	62.2	37	78.7	5	100.0	2	50.0	37	86.0
A national survey (e.g., NSSE, CCSSE, CIRP, EBI)	50	54.3	28	62.2	27	57.4	2	40.0	1	25.0	22	51.2
I don't know	0	0.0	1	2.2	0	0.0	0	0.0	0	0.0	0	0.0
Total	92	100.0	45	100.0	47	100.0	5	100.0	4	100.0	43	100.0

Table continues p. 126

Table continued from p. 125

Survey question/responses	Extended orientation seminar		Academic seminar: uniform content		Academic seminar: various topics		Preprofessional or discipline-linked seminar		Basic study skills seminar		Hybrid	
	Freq.	%	Freq.	%	Freq.	%	Freq.	%	Freq.	%	Freq.	%
Q76. Please identify the national survey(s) you used: (Select all that apply):												
Beginning College Survey of Student Engagement (BCSSE)	5	10.0	5	18.5	6	22.2	1	50.0	0	0.0	3	14.3
College Student Experiences Questionnaire (CSEQ)	0	0.0	0	0.0	0	0.0	0	0.0	0	0.0	0	0.0
Collegiate Learning Assessment (CLA)	4	8.0	3	11.1	6	22.2	0	0.0	0	0.0	4	19.0
Community College Survey of Student Engagement (CCSSE)	11	22.0	3	11.1	1	3.7	0	0.0	0	0.0	3	14.3
Cooperative Institutional Research Program (CIRP) Freshman Survey	12	24.0	6	22.2	13	48.1	1	50.0	0	0.0	3	14.3
Cooperative Institutional Research Program (CIRP) Your First College Year (YFCY) Survey	4	8.0	2	7.4	1	3.7	0	0.0	0	0.0	3	14.3
Faculty Survey of Student Engagement (FSSE)	2	4.0	2	7.4	4	14.8	0	0.0	1	100.0	2	9.5
First-Year Initiative (FYI)	9	18.0	3	11.1	1	3.7	0	0.0	0	0.0	0	0.0
Individual Developmental and Educational Assessment (IDEA)	1	2.0	0	0.0	3	11.1	0	0.0	0	0.0	2	9.5
National Survey of Student Engagement (NSSE)	35	70.0	21	77.8	22	81.5	2	100.0	1	100.0	16	76.2
Student Satisfaction Inventory (SSI)	9	18.0	3	11.1	2	7.4	0	0.0	1	100.0	3	14.3
Survey of Entering Student Engagement (SENSE)	1	2.0	1	3.7	0	0.0	0	0.0	0	0.0	0	0.0
Other (please specify)	6	12.0	4	14.8	4	14.8	1	50.0	0	0.0	6	28.6
Total	50	100.0	27	100.0	27	100.0	2	100.0	1	100.0	21	100.0

Survey question/responses	Extended orientation seminar		Academic seminar: uniform content		Academic seminar: various topics		Preprofessional or discipline-linked seminar		Basic study skills seminar		Hybrid	
	Freq.	%	Freq.	%	Freq.	%	Freq.	%	Freq.	%	Freq.	%
Q70. Please indicate each student outcome that was measured: (Select all that apply)												
Achievement of learning or course outcomes	114	64.8	55	67.1	60	71.4	10	71.4	7	63.6	54	79.4
Civic engagement	20	11.4	13	15.9	10	11.9	0	0.0	2	18.2	8	11.8
Connections with peers	70	39.8	26	31.7	29	34.5	3	21.4	3	27.3	26	38.2
Critical thinking	45	25.6	34	41.5	45	53.6	3	21.4	4	36.4	30	44.1
Grade point average	79	44.9	34	41.5	20	23.8	3	21.4	9	81.8	27	39.7
Information literacy	37	21.0	20	24.4	24	28.6	2	14.3	2	18.2	17	25.0
Involvement in service	25	14.2	9	11.0	4	4.8	1	7.1	4	36.4	10	14.7
Out-of-class student-faculty interaction	39	22.2	18	22.0	29	34.5	3	21.4	0	0.0	20	29.4
Participation in campus activities	74	42.0	25	30.5	22	26.2	1	7.1	3	27.3	26	38.2
Persistence to graduation	53	30.1	22	26.8	14	16.7	3	21.4	4	36.4	16	23.5
Persistence to second year	111	63.1	49	59.8	36	42.9	5	35.7	10	90.9	43	63.2
Satisfaction with advising	49	27.8	19	23.2	20	23.8	1	7.1	1	9.1	24	35.3
Satisfaction with faculty	76	43.2	47	57.3	49	58.3	7	50.0	4	36.4	47	69.1
Satisfaction with the seminar	135	76.7	60	73.2	62	73.8	10	71.4	7	63.6	56	82.4
Satisfaction with the institution	63	35.8	30	36.6	24	28.6	1	7.1	3	27.3	22	32.4
Student self-reports of course impact	78	44.3	44	53.7	39	46.4	4	28.6	6	54.5	42	61.8
Student self-reports of improvement	51	29.0	23	28.0	32	38.1	2	14.3	6	54.5	24	35.3
Understanding of institutional identity and culture	26	14.8	15	18.3	14	16.7	1	7.1	1	9.1	17	25.0
Use of campus services	69	39.2	24	29.3	16	19.0	1	7.1	3	27.3	26	38.2
Writing ability	17	9.7	26	31.7	40	47.6	1	7.1	2	18.2	15	22.1
Other (please specify)	10	5.7	4	4.9	8	9.5	2	14.3	0	0.0	5	7.4
Total	176	100.0	82	100.0	84	100.0	14	100.0	11	100.0	68	100.0

References

Astin, A. (1993). *What matters in college?: Four critical years revisited.* San Francisco, CA: Jossey-Bass.

Association of American Colleges & Universities (AAC&U), The National Leadership Council for Liberal Education & America's Promise. (2007). *College learning for the new global century.* Washington, DC: Author.

Attewell, P., Lavin, D., Domina, T., & Levey, T. (2006). New evidence on college remediation. *The Journal of Higher Education, 77*(5), 886–924.

Barefoot, B. O. (1992). *Helping first-year college students climb the academic ladder: Report of a national survey of freshman seminar programming in American higher education* (Unpublished doctoral dissertation). College of William and Mary, Williamsburg, VA.

Barefoot, B. O., & Fidler, P. P. (1996). *The 1994 National Survey of Freshmen Seminar Programs: Continuing innovations in the collegiate curriculum* (Monograph No. 20). Columbia, SC: University of South Carolina, National Resource Center for The Freshmen Year Experience & Students in Transition.

Barefoot, B. O., Griffin, B. Q., & Koch, A. K. (2012). *Enhancing student success and retention throughout undergraduate education: A national survey.* Brevard, NC: John N. Gardner Institute for Excellence in Undergraduate Education.

Borden, V. M. H. (2004). Accommodating student swirl: When traditional students are no longer the tradition. *Change, 36*(2), 10-17.

The Carnegie Foundation for the Advancement of Teaching. (n.d.). *Carnegie classification of institutions of higher education.* Retrieved from http://classifications.carnegiefoundation.org

Chickering, A. W., & Gamson, Z. F. (1987). Seven principles for good practice in undergraduate education. *AAHE Bulletin, 39*(7), 3-7.

Cuseo, J. B. (1991). *The freshman orientation seminar: A research-based rationale for its value, delivery, and content* (Monograph No. 4). Columbia, SC: University of South Carolina, National Resource Center for The Freshman Year Experience.

Eagan, M. K., & Jaeger, A. J. (2008). Closing the gate: Part-time faculty instruction in gatekeeper courses and first-year persistence. *New Directions for Teaching and Learning,* 115, 39-53.

Eagan, M. K., & Jaeger, A. J. (2009). Effects of exposure to part-time faculty on community college transfer. *Research in Higher Education, 50*(2), 168-188. doi:10.1007/s11162-008-9113-8

Eyler, J., & Giles, D. E. (1999). *Where's the learning in service-learning?* San Francisco, CA: Jossey-Bass.

Grosz, R. D. (1990). Suicide. *Journal of College Student Psychotherapy, 4*(3), 304-319.

Greenfield, G. M., Keup, J. R., & Gardner, J. N. (2013). *Developing and sustaining successful first-year programs: A guide for practitioners.* San Francisco, CA; Jossey-Bass.

Gunn, H. (2002, December). Web-based surveys: Changing the survey process. *First Monday, 7*(12). doi:10.5210/fm.v7i12.1014

Henscheid, J. M. (2004). First-year seminars in learning communities: Two reforms intersect. In J. M. Henscheid (Ed.), *Integrating the first-year experience: The role of learning communities in first-year seminars* (Monograph No. 39, pp. 1-8). Columbia, SC: University of South Carolina, National Resource Center for The First-Year Experience & Students in Transition.

Hill, R., & Reddy, P. (2007). Undergraduate peer mentoring: An investigation into processes, activities, and outcomes. *Psychology Learning & Teaching, 6*(2), 98-103.

Hunter, M. S., & Linder, C. W. (2005). First-year seminars. In M. L. Upcraft, J. N. Gardner, B. O. Barefoot, & Associates (Eds.), *Challenging and supporting the first-year student: A handbook for improving the first year of college.* (pp. 275-291). San Francisco, CA: Jossey-Bass.

Hurtado, S., & Carter, D. F. (1997). Effects of college transition and perceptions of the campus racial climate on Latino college students' sense of belonging. *Sociology of Education 70*(4), 324-345

Inkelas, K. K., & Longerbeam, S. D. (2008). Working toward a comprehensive typology of living-learning communities. In G. Luna & J. Gahagan (Eds.), *Learning initiatives in the residential setting* (Monograph No. 48, pp. 29-41). Columbia, SC: University of South Carolina, National Resource Center for The First-Year Experience & Students in Transition.

Jacobi, M. (1991). Mentoring and undergraduate academic success: A literature review. *Review of Educational Research, 61*, 505-532.

Jaeger, A. J. (2008). Contingent faculty and student outcomes. *Academe, 94*(6), 42-43.

Kinzie, J. (February, 2013). *Foster, sustain and improve quality in the first college year: Creating magical processes and making dreams … reality.* Keynote speech presented at the 32nd Annual Conference on the First-Year Experience, Orlando, FL.

Kram, K. E., & Isabella, L. A. (1985). Mentoring alternatives: The role of peer relationships in career development. *The Academy of Management Journal, 28,* 110-132.

Kuh, G. D. (2008). *High-impact educational practices: What they are, who has access to them, and why they matter.* Washington, DC: Association of American Colleges and Universities.

Kuh, G. D. (2010). High-impact practices: Retrospective and prospective. In J. E. Brownell & L. E. Swaner, *Five high-impact practices: Research on learning outcomes, completion, and quality.* (pp. v-xiii). Washington, DC: Association of American Colleges & Universities.

Kuh, G. D., Kinzie, J., Schuh, J. H., Whitt, E. J., & Associates. (2005). *Student success in college: Creating conditions that matter.* San Francisco, CA: Jossey-Bass.

Landrum, R. E., & Nelson, L. R. (2002). The undergraduate research assistantship: An analysis of the benefits. *Teaching of Psychology, 29*(1), 15-19.

Laufgraben, J. L. (2006). *Common reading programs: Going beyond the book* (Monograph No. 44). Columbia, SC: University of South Carolina, National Resource Center for The First-Year Experience & Students in Transition.

Lenning, O. T., & Ebbers, L. H. (1999). *The powerful potential of learning communities: Improving education for the future.* (ASHE-ERIC Higher Education Report No. 26-6). Washington, DC: The George Washington University, Graduate School of Education and Human Development.

Leskes, A., & Miller, R. E. (2006). *Purposeful pathways: Helping students achieve key learning outcomes.* Washington, DC: Association of American Colleges and Universities.

Lewis, S. E., & Lewis, J. E. (2005). Departing from lectures: An evaluation of a peer-led guided inquiry alternative. *Journal of Chemical Education, 82*(1), 135-140.

Love, A. G., & Tokuno, K. A. (1999). Learning community models. In J. H. Levine (Ed.), *Learning communities: New structures, new partnerships for learning* (Monograph No. 26, pp. 9–18). Columbia, SC: University of South Carolina, National Resource Center for The First-Year Experience & Students in Transition.

MacGregor, J., Smith, B. L., Matthews, R. S., & Gabelnick, F. (1990). Learning community models. *New Directions for Teaching and Learning, 41*, 19–37. doi:10.1002/tl.37219904104

Morse, R., & Flanigan, S. (2012, September 11). How *U.S. News* calculates its best colleges rankings. *U.S. News & World Report.* Retrieved from www.usnews.com

National Center for Education Statistics. (2013). *Integrated postsecondary education data system* [Data file]. Retrieved from http://nces.ed.gov/ipeds

National Resource Center for The First-Year Experience & Students in Transition. (2002). *The 2000 National Survey of First-Year Seminar Programs: Continuing innovations in the collegiate curriculum* (Monograph No. 35). Columbia, SC: University of South Carolina, Author.

Nora, A., & Crisp, G. (2007). Mentoring students: Conceptualizing and validating the multi-dimensions of a support system. *Journal of College Student Retention: Research, Theory & Practice, 9*, 337-356.

Padgett, R. D., & Keup, J. R. (2011). *2009 National Survey of First-Year Seminars: Ongoing efforts to support students in transition* (Research Reports on College Transitions No. 2). Columbia, SC: University of South Carolina, National Resource Center for The First-Year Experience & Students in Transition.

Pascarella, E. T., & Terenzini, P. T. (2005). *How college affects students, Vol. 2: A third decade of research.* San Francisco, CA: Jossey-Bass.

Provasnik, S., & Planty, M. (2008). *Community colleges: Special supplement to the condition of education 2008: Statistical analysis report* (Report No. NCES 2008-033). Washington, DC: National Center for Education Statistics.

Schuster, J. H., & Finkelstein, M. J. (2006). *The American faculty: The restructuring of academic work and careers.* Baltimore, MD: The Johns Hopkins University Press.

Schuster, J. H., & Finkelstein, M. J. (2007). *On the brink: Assessing the status of American faculty* (CSHE Research & Occasional Paper No. CSHE.3.07). Retrieved from University of California, Berkeley, Center for Studies in Higher Education website: http://escholarship.org/uc/item/1ch73352

Shapiro, N. S., & Levine, J. H. (1999). *Creating learning communities: A practical guide to winning support, organizing for change, and implementing programs.* San Francisco, CA: Jossey-Bass.

Sharkin, B. S., Plageman, P. M., & Mangold, S. L. (2003). College student response to peers in distress: An exploratory study. *Journal of College Student Development, 44*(5), 691-698.

Skipper, T. L., & Keup, J. R. (2010, March). *The 2009 National Survey on First-Year Seminars: Innovations in the undergraduate curriculum.* Presentation given at the 2010 ACPA Convention, Boston, MA.

Snider, K. J. G., & Venable, A. M. (May, 2000). *Assessing learning community effectiveness: A multi-campus approach.* Presentation given at the 2000 Association for Institutional Research Annual Forum, Cincinnati, OH.

Stassen, M. L. A. (2003). Student outcomes: The impact of varying living-learning community models. *Research in Higher Education, 44*(5), 581-613.

Tinto, V. (1993). *Leaving college: Rethinking the causes and cures of student attrition* (2nd ed.). Chicago, IL: University of Chicago Press.

Tobolowsky, B. F. (2005). *The 2003 National Survey of First-Year Seminars: Continuing innovations in the collegiate curriculum* (Monograph No. 41). Columbia, SC: University of South Carolina, National Resource Center for The First-Year Experience & Students in Transition.

Tobolowsky, B. F., & Associates. (2008). *2006 National Survey of First-Year Seminars: Continuing innovations in the collegiate curriculum* (Monograph No. 51). Columbia, SC: University of South Carolina, National Resource Center for The First-Year Experience & Students in Transition.

Umbach, P. D. (2007). How effective are they? Exploring the impact of contingent faculty on undergraduate education. *The Review of Higher Education, 30*(2), 91-123.

Upcraft, M. L., Gardner, J. N., Barefoot, B. O., & Associates. (2005). *Challenging and supporting the first-year student: A handbook for improving the first year of college.* San Francisco, CA: Jossey-Bass.

Wang, M. C., Dziuban, C. D., & Moskal, P. D. (2000). A web-based survey system for distributed learning impact evaluation. *The Internet and Higher Education, 2*(4), 211-220. doi:10.1016/S1096-7516(00)00021-X

Wingspread Group on Higher Education. (1993). An American imperative: Higher expectations for higher education. Racine, WI: Johnson Foundation.

Zlotkowski, E. (Ed.). (2002). *Service-learning and the first-year experience: Preparing students for personal success and civic responsibility* (Monograph No. 34). Columbia, SC: University of South Carolina, National Resource Center for The First-Year Experience & Students in Transition.

About the Authors

Dallin George Young is the assistant director for research, grants, and assessment at the National Resource Center for The First-Year Experience and Students in Transition. He coordinates the research and assessment endeavors of the National Resource Center and facilitates and disseminates three national surveys: the National Survey of First-Year Seminars, the National Survey of Sophomore-Year Initiatives, and the National Survey of Senior Capstone Experiences. He oversees a number of research collaborations and grant opportunities between the National Resource Center and the higher education community and across the University of South Carolina campus. Before joining the Center, Young worked in administrative roles in college student housing and assessment. He has taught sections of University 101, a first-year seminar for students at South Carolina. He holds a bachelor's degree in liberal arts and sciences from Utah State University, a master's degree in higher education and student affairs from Virginia Tech, and a doctorate in college student affairs administration from the University of Georgia. Young's research interests have led to publications and presentations on learning outcomes of postsecondary professional preparation, peer leadership, the impact of professional standards in higher education, and assessment.

Jessica Hopp is the graduate assistant for research, grants, and assessment at the National Resource Center for The First-Year Experience and Students in Transition at the University of South Carolina. Currently, she is a second-year student in the Higher Education and Student Affairs master's program at South Carolina. She serves as co-instructor for the University 101 first-year seminar course. Hopp holds bachelor's degrees in human development and psychology from the University of Wisconsin-Green Bay (UWGB). While at UWGB, she was a peer mentor for a first-year seminar course, which led to a research opportunity with then advisor, Dr. Denise Bartell, exploring first-year seminar outcomes; retention; and the effects of first-year student, instructor, and peer mentor relationships.